# We Built the Wall

# We Built the Wall

*How the US Keeps Out Asylum Seekers
from Mexico, Central America and Beyond*

Eileen Truax

*Translated by Diane Stockwell*

**VERSO**
London • New York

First published by Verso 2018
© Eileen Truax 2018
Translation © Diane Stockwell 2018

1 3 5 7 9 10 8 6 4 2

**Verso**
UK: 6 Meard Street, London W1F 0EG
US: 20 Jay Street, Suite 1010, Brooklyn, NY 11201

versobooks.com

Verso is the imprint of New Left Books

ISBN-13: 978-1-78663-217-3
ISBN-13: 978-1-78663-216-6 (US EBK)
ISBN-13: 978-1-78663-215-9 (UK EBK)

**British Library Cataloguing in Publication Data**
A catalogue record for this book is available from the British Library

**Library of Congress Cataloging-in-Publication Data**
A catalog record for this book is available from the Library of Congress

Typeset in Fournier MT by Hewer Text UK Ltd, Edinburgh
Printed in the U.S. by Maple Press

For my fellow journalists in Mexico. For those who died denouncing injustice, and for those who have been persecuted and killed for telling their stories.

And for the lawyers in the United States who work pro bono to save lives.

# Contents

# Acknowledgments

One night in December 2012, José Luis Benavides, Kent Kirkton, and Julián Cardona came over to my house. They had barely walked in the door before Benavides said, "I have the story for your next book." That book is *We Built The Wall*.

I made my first trip to El Paso and Juárez in early 2013, and I would go two more times over the next two years. There, I discovered the generosity and clarity of purpose of Carlos, Sandra, and Alejandra Spector, and the boundless courage of those they represent, overcoming their fear, anger, and indignation to rebuild their lives, while continuing to demand justice.

Thanks to Sara Salazar de Reyes, Saúl Reyes, Gloria López, and their families, for opening their homes and their hearts to me. To Martín Huéramo, Carlos Gutiérrez, Alejandro Hernández Pacheco, Cipriana Jurado, Sandra Rodríguez Nieto, Irma Casas, Rubén García, Arturo Bañuelas, Claudia Amaro, and Yamil Yáujar; sisters Nitza,

Mitzi, and Deisy Alvarado; Rocío Hernández, Santiago García, Erick Midence, and Enrique Morones, for sharing moments from their lives, their experience, and their knowledge of both sides of the border. To Melissa del Bosque, Julián Cardona, and Marcela Turati for their extraordinary documentation work, and to my journalist colleagues at *El Diario de Juárez* for being a beacon of light to better understand life in the complex El Paso–Juárez region. To immigration lawyer Daniel M. Kowalsi for sharing information necessary to understand the tangled web of U.S. immigration law.

To Diane Stockwell, I owe gratitude not only for her complicity and energy in getting this book published, but also for her sensitivity in understanding that every word spoken by a victim of forced migration has meaning. To Andrew Hsiao and the team at Verso Books, I am grateful to you for raising the voices of the protagonists in this book so they will reach those who have yet to hear them.

Thanks to Edgar Krauss, Alfredo Corchado, and Angela Kocherga, for their encouragement at the beginning of this project, and to Willivaldo Delgadillo and Toni Piqué for their critical readings. To Jaime Abello Banfi, Natalia Algarín, and the Fundación Nuevo Periodismo's journalistic books workshop for giving me the chance to work on the first draft of this book under the masterful watch of Martín Caparrós. To Diego Fonseca, Catalina Lobo-Guerrero, Ander Izagirre, Roberto Valencia, Claudia Jardim, Andrés Hernández, Esteban Castro, and Cecilia Lanza, for their thoughtful readings and incisive critiques.

José Luis Benavides and Kent Kirkton have my admiration and warm appreciation for their intelligence and ability to feel injustice against others as if it were theirs—and my gratitude for making room for me in their little red pickup truck and taking me along on their tour through the borderlands.

A few days before New Year's Eve in 2013, Diego Sedano and I got into our car and set off for Fabens, Texas, to go talk to Saúl Reyes and his family. A year later, we drove even further, from Los Angeles to San Antonio, to talk to the three young sisters who still hope their mother will come back one day. For the stories, the tears, and the songs we shared on those days driving down Highway 10, this is Diego's book, too.

# Introduction

Ann Donnelly's name echoed all over social media the night of January 28, 2017. Donnelly had been a federal district court judge for just over a year when a ruling from her court in Brooklyn, New York, made her the first judge to block an executive order by President Donald Trump.

The executive order, signed by Trump the day before on Friday, January 27, was announced as a temporary cancellation of permission to enter the United States for citizens of seven countries: Libya, Syria, Iraq, Iran, Sudan, Yemen, and Somalia, with the alleged aim of protecting the country from terrorism. Although the order defined those barred from entering by their nationality, it was widely known as the "Muslim ban," a phrase popularized by Trump himself during his presidential campaign, because Islam was the predominant religion in the seven countries cited.

Of the twenty-three executive orders signed by Trump during his first twelve weeks in office, this was the most polemic, stirring the strongest reaction from U.S. citizens.

Within just a few hours, large crowds descended on the biggest airports in the country to protest the measure and to show support for people being detained upon arrival, including permanent U.S. residents who had temporarily traveled to their country of origin. Syrian refugees scheduled to arrive in the United States that weekend were detained; an infant girl from Iran traveling to the United States for life-saving heart surgery was not allowed to enter the country. Within a few days, federal courts in other cities had also blocked the order. For the first time in many years, the United States took a hard look at itself and its policies of accepting and excluding refugees, asylum seekers, immigrants, and people from other countries in general.

It was probably about time. For decades, the United States has promoted itself to the rest of the world as a democratic country, with an open-arms policy that affirms diversity, which has very little to do with how the nation actually shapes its policies around immigration, refuge, and asylum.

In spite of being the country with the largest number of immigrants in the world—almost 50 million people living in U.S. territory were not born there—the United States has a smaller percentage of immigrants in relation to the general population than other countries. Immigrants comprise 14 percent of the U.S. population, compared with 22 percent in Canada and 28 percent in Australia; countries that have openly acknowledged their need for foreign labor have reached figures as high as 75 percent in Qatar and 88 percent in the United Arab Emirates. Even in Spain, a country experiencing large-scale immigration only recently, 13 percent of the population are immigrants, just one percentage point less than the United States.

Another image the United States sells to the world is the "melting pot," referring to its ethnic diversity. Compared with other countries, however, it is not a leader in that sense either. In terms of diversity, once again other countries such as Canada, Denmark, and the United Kingdom have higher indices. In the United States, one of every four immigrants comes from a single country, Mexico. In other destination countries popular with immigrants, mainly in Europe, migration comes from a wider, more diverse range of countries.

As with most countries that receive immigrants, the current demographic composition of the United States is the result of the government's application of immigration policy based on the country's economic and workplace needs. But it is also a function of the alliances and shifting sands of international politics. In terms of refuge and asylum policy, and the methods for detaining and processing immigrants, the predominant principles have more to do with political, and even partisan, criteria, not human rights or social justice. The United States opens its arms to whoever benefits it economically at the moment, and to asylum and refuge seekers who can demonstrate persecution or a threat to their safety or their lives, as long as they come from countries with governments viewed as questionable by the United States. For those seeking asylum or refuge for identical reasons who come from countries with governments viewed as friendly and democratic by the United States, the door slams shut, even if they can demonstrate a fear for their lives as credible as any exhibited by nationalities with governments deemed hostile by the U.S.

Throughout history, the collective imagination of the United States has constructed the "other" as the enemy—"the undesirable," as described by law professor Bill Ong Hing. That "other" has evolved as necessary to successive administrations. There was "the undesirable Asian"—Chinese, Japanese, Filipinos—in the second half of the nineteenth century, followed by Jews and Italians at the beginning of the twentieth century, Communists for several decades, Mexicans for much of the same century, Central Americans for the last twenty years, and Muslims filling the role of the "other" for the first decades of the twenty-first century.

The normalization of using political criteria to establish rules for entering the country, and for granting refugee status or political asylum in particular, is reflected in actions such as Trump's order, which broadly violates international protocols protecting human rights.

After glimpsing a reflection of itself as a nation in the "Muslim ban," a significant part of the U.S. public has reacted with horrified alarm; along with protests in the streets, a strong legal response has been launched. Just hours after Trump's executive order was announced, groups of volunteer lawyers got to work, setting up shop in airport cafeterias. The American Civil Liberties Union (ACLU), the most powerful civil rights organization in the country, filed its first lawsuit in the name of two brothers originally from Iraq in the federal court presided over by Judge Donnelly, resulting in the first suspension of the travel ban. That Monday, barely seventy-two hours after Trump's executive order was signed and suspended, the ACLU reported that it had received $24 million in donations in just three days through its website—six times more than the total for an average year.

One hallmark of Donald Trump's presidential campaign was connecting anti-terrorist and national security rhetoric with migration. In addition to justifying measures like the "Muslim ban," such connections encompassed building a border wall, accusing Mexicans of being drug dealers and rapists, and claiming without evidence that undocumented people vote illegally; these last two assertions reinforced his promise to deport 11 million undocumented people from the country.

Since he was sworn into office, reality has forced Trump to tone down this rhetoric. During his administration's first hundred days, the "Muslim ban" was blocked twice. The 11 million promised deportees has shrunk to 2 or 3 million; given the state of U.S. infrastructure and federal resources, deporting such a massive number of people would be extremely difficult and onerous, aside from incurring political and social costs. As for the border wall, Congress has forced Trump to get his head out of the clouds. The political will may be there and the legislative grounds in place, but at least for the first two fiscal years of the Trump administration, the money has not been included in the budget.

With no way to launch a controlled media offensive on these issues—not even by disqualifying them as "fake news"—and faced with the need to produce some evidence of success in his first months in office, Trump seems to have chosen to focus his efforts on arresting undocumented people and putting them into deportation proceedings, as well as denying entry to people seeking refuge or political asylum in the United States. Neither action requires any special allocation of resources, or Congressional approval.

Although talking about Trump as a dangerous threat to immigrants has been a good strategy for media outlets trying to increase their online traffic, the so-called "deportation machine" has already been up and running for at least a decade, beginning with the George W. Bush administration in 2001 in the wake of the 9/11 terrorist attacks, and picking up steam during Barack Obama's time in office. Almost 3 million people were deported in the eight years of Obama's presidency—a number that Trump has provided as a possible goal for his administration. And the criteria in place for granting refuge or asylum were established fifty years ago, initially based on international humanitarian goals but implemented in the service of convenience and political interests.

This book aims to lay bare these two phenomena. U.S. immigration policy during the Trump presidency and in the years beyond could be outrageous and appalling, but discriminatory policy is nothing new. Most Americans have refused to acknowledge that the immigrant community has endured discrimination and a hostile environment for decades. Tax dollars paid by U.S. residents are spent to lock up immigrants, re-victimizing those who have already been victimized in their home countries, who have reached out to "the best democracy in the world" in an attempt to save their own lives. Those who come to the United States fleeing violence, or for health reasons, or to escape hate and harassment because of their sexual orientation or religious beliefs have been forgotten by their home countries. But in the United States, we have not done much better. We rarely think about the new arrivals who have had to leave everything behind and come here as a last resort, arriving in a new land only to be labeled "the other," the foreigner, and whose lives depend on accepting this description. From the comfort of our own secure legal status, we have already built the Wall.

In Part One, I will present a general overview of the hundreds of thousands of victims of violence who arrive in the United States each year seeking asylum and the series of obstacles, including bureaucratic red tape, a confounding legal system, and social indifference, they meet here. I will discuss how the southern border of the United States has functioned as a port of entry for those whose presence in the country ultimately benefits the government, while this same border has also served to reinforce the concept of "the other."

Part Two offers a deeper analysis of how the criteria for granting and denying asylum were developed. I also examine the robust business these criteria represent for the corporations that manage private immigration detention centers. In Part Three, I talk about the governments of Mexico and other countries that not only have failed to meet their responsibility to ensure the safety and well-being of their citizens, but also are at times complicit in the violence and persecution that compels people to leave. Finally, in Part Four I will tell the stories of those who have had to start their lives all over again in the United States, a completely unknown land, to the great indifference of most of its residents.

The stories told in this book only hint at the enormous debt the United States owes to its own image as a democratic country, and the role it plays in human rights violations committed around the world, including in Mexico. My hope is that through reading this book, people inside and outside the United States can knock down the wall of indifference that we have propped up for years, and offer understanding and solidarity to the most courageous among us: those who have risked their lives to denounce injustice, to defend what they believe in, and who, years later, with tremendous strength, have learned to live again.

# Part One
# The Border

# 1

# The Line Between Life and Death

The desert is wily. With every breeze, dust wafts across the highway leading into town, a fine sand that clings to cars, to your shoes, to your tongue. Lines of desert sand run along the edges of the streets, separating the pavement from the simple ranch houses, painted in earth tones, surrounded by chicken-wire fences. In some yards small trees struggle to grow, defying the arid conditions, surrounded by tricycles and clothes hung on lines to dry in the sun. It feels like we're in Guadalupe, in Juárez Valley, Chihuahua, Mexico; the Church of the Nazarene, the tortilla stand at the supermarket, the hand-lettered signs advertising home-cooked meals all add to the illusion. But before turning around on the highway, right where the desert ends and the row of humble little houses begins, a small, unassuming sign tells you where you are: Fabens, Texas.

A nine-mile stretch bisected by the Río Grande separates Fabens from Guadalupe, along the U.S.-Mexico border, a thirty-minute drive east of the bridge connecting El Paso and Juárez, Mexico. Lower Island Avenue on this side of the border becomes Cruz Reyes Street on the other. Just beyond a sign reading, "Estados Unidos Mexicanos," another row of houses begins, a mirror image of the first: the same colors, the same stunted trees, the same sand swept across the road, the same first names, the same last names. The difference is that in Guadalupe, the homes are empty. The people who lived there were killed. The ones left alive were threatened, extorted, mutilated. They grabbed a few belongings when they could, crossed the border, and never went back.

The ones who managed to get out of Guadalupe alive arrived in Fabens with nothing. They don't speak English, they have no savings, no furniture, no property, no papers. Some don't even have an old family photo album. They came to Fabens with nothing more than their beating hearts—no dreams, no plans beyond the simple will to survive.

The distance between Fabens and Guadalupe is the distance between life and death.

On New Year's Eve, 2013, the Reyes house glows with light. Saúl Reyes, his wife Gloria, his children, his mother Sara, and six or seven close friends have gathered for dinner. Saúl lives in this little residential enclave in the middle of the desert, in Fabens, but just like the rest of his family, his home will always be on the Mexico side, in Guadalupe. He fled north to survive. The Reyes Salazar family, a clan of bakers with a long history of social activism, resisted leaving their hometown. But out of ten siblings, four of them men, Saúl Reyes Salazar and three of his sisters are the only ones still living. Two died of natural causes. Four were murdered.

The members of the Reyes Salazar family had been militant leftists for decades. They belonged to various organizations and political parties that sprang up across Mexico in the sixties: from the Popular Defense Committee (CDP) and the Unified Socialist Party of Mexico (PSUM) to the still-functioning Revolutionary Democratic Party (PRD). Eusebio Reyes, a baker and the family patriarch, was born in Torreón, Coahuila, a state bordering Texas. After trying to organize his fellow bakers to demand better working conditions, he was fired, and no one else would hire him. He decided to move away, and wound up in Guadalupe. He opened his own bakery and taught his children the trade, while imparting lessons in worker solidarity and social activism.

In the early nineties, the Reyeses led a resistance movement against a proposed nuclear waste dump in Sierra Blanca, Texas, nine miles north of the Mexican border and Juárez Valley. On March 21, 1992, along with other local activist groups, they held a protest called "Marcha por la Vida" (March for Life), which advanced towards Sierra Blanca from El Paso and both sides of the border, to highlight the rights of border communities to a safe environment free of pollution.

Saúl, in his forties and about average height, has a ruddy, dark complexion. With a sharp gaze and a tendency to get right to the point, he is serious, attentive. But when he looks back on the protest, he smiles proudly. They shut down every border crossing in the area for an entire hour.

"It was the first time in history anything like that was ever done," he points out. As a result of the wave of protests, the Sierra Blanca nuclear waste project was canceled. Years later some attempts were made to revive it, with no success.

The Reyes family came to symbolize the fight to protect the environment against big corporations and U.S. interests, in a part of Mexico that had never seemed to matter much to the rest of the country or the federal government. Over the years, the family was active in a variety of causes: constructing homes in Juárez Valley for people who had tried unsuccessfully to cross into the United States; protesting the killing of women in the area, an issue that Josefina, one of Saúl's sisters, worked on the most; fighting to improve conditions for factory workers in Juárez; and protesting the militarization of the area that began in 2008 as part of an operation by the Mexican federal government to combat narcotrafficking, and which included a wave of repression and human rights violations.

People who knew the Reyes family recall the four brothers—Eleazar, Elías, Saúl, and Rubén—working together at the bakery and at the small chain of stores that the family owned. One kneaded the dough while another shaped it into loaves, the third prepared pastries, and the fourth took bread out of the oven. As they worked, they would discuss issues in the residential development they had built and politics in Juárez Valley. Sometimes they would go out to deliver the bread, or serve pastries to customers, along with a cup of coffee.

On that New Year's Eve, December 31, 2013, Saúl falls back on an old custom. He gets home at around nine o'clock, when dinner is almost ready. He has brought with him a traditional Reyes, or "king's" cake—which in this case is aptly named for two reasons—that he baked for his family himself. He had started working at a bakery in Fabens as soon as he got there, earning eight dollars an hour. This is what he knows, and he's good at it, but now he's alone. All that remains of his brothers are memories.

The string of Reyes murders started on August 23, 2008. Josefina and other activists had organized a march to protest the military's presence in the Juárez Valley. A week later, a group of soldiers kidnapped her younger son, Miguel Angel. After two weeks of demonstrations outside military installations, and a hunger strike by Josefina, Miguel Angel was released with two fractured ribs, a broken nose, and signs of torture from electric shocks delivered to the soles of his feet.[1] Three months later, men wearing masks and armed with guns burst into an event hall where a wedding reception was being held, searched among the guests, and killed Josefina's oldest son, Julio César. They shot him through the heart. He was nineteen years old.

Instead of keeping quiet, the Reyeses kept up their activism. They demanded justice for Julio César and the army's withdrawal from Guadalupe and Juárez Valley. On January 3, 2010, Josefina Reyes was killed when she stopped to get something to eat while driving home from her mother's house. In August 2010, her brother Rubén Reyes was gunned down in the street, in broad daylight. On February 7, 2011, Malena Reyes, Elías Reyes, and his wife Luisa Ornelas were kidnapped. A week after the kidnapping, while Sara, the matriarch of the family, was protesting in front of the statehouse in Chihuahua, the state's capital, her house was burned to the ground. On February 26, the dead bodies of the three kidnapping victims were found. An onslaught of threats to the family followed.

In spite of his earlier resolve not to give in to threats, Saúl understood that the time to leave had come. The family left everything behind: the comfortable home Saúl and Gloria had built themselves, brick by brick; their family bakery passed down to him by his mother; the books Saúl had read with his siblings as they made bread; all of their belongings. As soon as Saúl, Gloria, and their three children fled Guadalupe in April 2011, their house and the bakery were broken into and burned to the ground. Sara, his mother, crossed the border the following December.

"We didn't want to leave. We had been taught that we had to fight for our country, and we knew that our country was in a bad way, but we wanted to stay to make it better," Saúl Reyes explained when I talked to him for the first time in El Paso. "When I go to give a talk at the universities and they ask me why I came, I tell them I didn't just come here, they pushed me out."

Saúl was granted political asylum in January 2012, and in the coming months around thirty Reyes family members started the process of applying for asylum. The family's story traveled around the world as a devastating example of the persecution and extreme violence endured by ordinary individuals and the tragic impunity enjoyed by criminals in Mexico.

In 2008 Operation Chihuahua went into effect, an initiative of then-president Felipe Calderón's administration aiming to dismantle organized crime in that state. In its first phase, the program dispatched roughly 10,000 military and federal police personnel to Chihuahua, claiming that these forces of law and order would take control of the state. Meanwhile, the local municipal and state police forces would be "cleansed" of their connections to drug cartels. The Sinaloa cartel, the Juárez cartel (known as "La Linea"), and the Zetas were all at war over territory and had been accused of murdering police chiefs who formed alliances with rival drug gangs. During the operation's second phase, the newly installed local police would be trained, and the state would be left under their control. But according to official data and claims by human rights groups, kidnappings, extortion, breaking and entering, and murders became even worse during the years when the operation was in effect.

Not even four months had passed since the operation began when Carlos Spector, an immigration lawyer in El Paso, began to be approached by activists and journalists from Chihuahua seeking political asylum in the United States. The exodus began with Emilio Gutiérrez, a journalist from Ascención, Chihuahua. He was followed by Cipriana Jurado, who in 2011 became the first human rights activist to have an asylum petition approved by the United States. Asylum seeker Marisol Valles, police chief of the Práxedis G. Guerrero municipality, was dubbed "the bravest woman in Mexico." Carlos Gutiérrez, a married father of two, refused to pay the extortion "quota" for his catering business; his feet were sawed off in the back of his car as punishment. Incredibly, he survived, although both legs had to be amputated below the knee. In 2014, using prosthetic legs, Gutiérrez launched a bike caravan that traveled across Texas to the governor's mansion in Austin to demand justice for the victims of violence in Mexico.

Newspapers in Mexico and around the world published stories on Carlos's clients. One, then another, then another came to ask for his help, until the protagonists of perhaps the most emblematic case of all those exiled by violence in Juárez Valley made their way to Carlos's office: the Reyes Salazar family.

After leaving Guadalupe, Saúl and his family made their way to El Paso and stayed at a shelter for migrants and the homeless. Neither Saúl nor Gloria spoke any English. Their children—thirteen, six, and three years old—would have to attend a school program for English language learners. Saúl took whatever work he could get, from gardening and yard work to unpacking fresh produce at a supermarket. They found a small apartment, which, with a little effort, could accommodate the five of them and Sara, who had arrived by then. A few months later Saúl heard that rents were much cheaper in Fabens, about a half hour east of El Paso, and that there were other people from Guadalupe there. The family moved, and Saúl found a new job.

The Reyes family has tried to make a fresh start and adapt to a new life in a mobile home in the middle of the Texas desert. According to the most recent census figures available, of 8,250 residents in Fabens, 97 percent are Latino and 90 percent are Mexican. That figure is from 2010 and a large part of the exodus caused by violence only began that year; it is hard to say, therefore, how much the population has grown or changed in composition since then.[2] A walk through Fabens's sandy streets indicates that many of the people living here arrived recently: about a third of the homes are not houses but mobile homes or trailers— "*trailas*," as they are known in local parlance.

People in the same circumstances as Saúl live in these trailers. They do not have the financial resources to buy a plot of land or a house, and monthly rent payments on an apartment are too burdensome. Renting a trailer is cheaper, and although space is tight, trailers come equipped with the basic necessities: a small kitchen area with a gas stove, a bathroom, electricity, and divided rooms. Saúl has a trailer on a corner lot, enclosed by a fence. The trailer is not in great shape, but it's a good size, big enough to house separate, though small, rooms for his mother and his children. The dining room table is at the heart of the trailer.

As guests arrive in the final hours of 2013, more chairs are placed around the table. Saúl greets everyone as they enter the trailer, making them feel welcome. In comes Martín Huéramo, forty-six, a trusted political ally of the Reyes brothers back in Guadalupe, and like a brother to Saúl. When the Reyes family moved to Fabens in 2013, Martín was already there. With a powerful build, a complexion tanned from the sun, and a thick mustache framing a gentle smile, Martín had been doing well in Guadalupe. His family, originally from Michoacán, had moved to Guadalupe when he was just a boy. Like everyone who grew up in Juárez Valley then, Martín remembers a time of plenty, when hard work paid off. Skilled in construction, Martín built himself three houses in Guadalupe. He sold one in order to come to Fabens.

"They weren't fancy houses, just the typical kind of house in Juárez Valley," he says, humbly. Martín wears a checkered shirt typical of the working-class men in the area, and even though he has lived in Texas for three years, when he talks his accent is 100 percent Chihuahua.

Since he had always owned the houses where he lived, Martín set about searching for a plot of land to build a house on when he arrived in the United States. But a few days into his search, he got the first hard dose of reality that often greets new arrivals: the value of Mexican currency plummets the minute you cross the border.

"What had been my whole life's work had no value here," Martín explains, dejected. "I was basically illiterate, I didn't know the language and I couldn't write. I had to start all over, like a child."

A few minutes before the clock strikes midnight, as the women put the final touches on the meal, Saúl and Martín talk. Martín comments on the sheer magnitude of the migration from Juárez to El Paso. Because of the politics specific to border cities, many people on the Mexican side have a document that allows them to cross back and forth. Others are U.S. citizens or have children who are. In the face of growing violence and the resulting crisis in Juárez Valley and in the capital city of Chihuahua, people are coming over to El Paso and deciding to stay put. The effects of the growing numbers of exiles have become apparent within just a few months, Martín says, including overcrowding in schools from the influx of new students and heavier traffic on the highways connecting El Paso to the surrounding suburbs.

One of those suburbs is Fabens. It's something of a paradox that, of all the places to migrate, these natives of Guadalupe have settled in a town that's the mirror image of where they came from. When I ask Saúl and Martín if the similarity convinced them to stay in Fabens, they both smile. Saúl assures me that they live in Fabens simply because it's cheaper than other places.

I met Sara Salazar de Reyes for the first time in a Chinese restaurant in El Paso, the same day I met Saúl, Gloria, and their children. Doña Sara was seventy-nine, with a vacant stare. She is polite and smiles cordially to everyone, but her eyes are blank—the emptiness death leaves behind.

Almost a year later, I see Sara for the second time, at the New Year's dinner at Saúl's trailer home. At the stroke of midnight we are all sitting around the table, with Saúl's *rosca de reyes*, or three kings' bread, which he baked that afternoon at the supermarket bakery where he works. As the head of the family, Saúl thanks everyone for their friendship and for coming to dinner. He also gives thanks simply for being alive, and says that he hopes the new year will be the best one yet. The clock strikes twelve, announcing the arrival of 2014, and everyone starts hugging each other. Doña Sara goes over to a little side table to look at some family photos displayed there and starts to cry. She does not stop for quite a while. A decorative wall hanging reads, "The love of a family is life's greatest blessing." Later, Sara tells me that when her son Eleazar was diagnosed with cancer, she told everyone, "It is forbidden to die before I do."

The next morning everyone gets together again for a breakfast of leftovers from the night before, and Gloria cooks some more. The women play dominoes at the table, while Doña Sara invites me to come back to her little room to talk. There, surrounded by photos of all of her children, she tells me about each one of them. Her daughter Elba died in childbirth, and Sara raised Elba's son, Ismael, like one of her own. Rubén, her son, was a good man; he had been walking to the store to buy milk for his workers when he was killed. Josefina was closest to her mother; Sara went along with her to the demonstrations, the protests, the meetings with other activists. "Just imagine, me and my daughter are having coffee, and just an hour later they tell me she has been killed. It was very hard," she says, letting out a sob.

Sara tells me how painful it was to see Saúl in those first days of exile. When she first arrived in El Paso, the family was still living in a shelter. "When I got there, I found my son eating a piece of stale bread," she says. "It broke my heart."

"I always went along with my children in everything we did," she recalls of the family's activism in Mexico. "After they killed my grandson, we stepped up protests against the police, the soldiers. When the soldiers came, that's when our martyrdom began. We started to protest, to get people together to demand the soldiers be withdrawn, but my children started to fall." She weeps openly. "The last thing, which was hardest for me, was the kidnapping of Elías and Malena. I don't mean it wasn't hard with my other children—as each one fell, a piece of my heart was lost—but with them I had nothing left."

Sara had not wanted to come to the United States, but had been left without a choice when Saúl began receiving threats. "If you stay here, they're going to come after you to find out where I am," Saúl told her. Now she says she probably would not return to Mexico. "We don't have anything left there anymore," she says. "They burned it all down."

Through Doña Sara's window you can see laundry hanging out to dry on the clotheslines. On sunny days, like that New Year's Day in 2014, the clothes dry quickly. But when the wind picks up and gusts from the south, everything gets covered in dust. The desert is wily.

# 2

# Carlos Spector, Attorney-at-Law for Impossible Cases

I first meet Carlos Spector, a lawyer, in early 2013 at ¡Ándale!, a restaurant in El Paso with a logo of a fat man in a sombrero eating tacos. Stepping inside is like walking into a garish street fair, with fake cast-iron bars over fake windows and fake serenades. An overweight Joan Sebastian impersonator performs for a sparse audience, who silently beg him to stop. Carlos's wife Sandra greets me warmly at the door, and we look for a table as far as possible from the "entertainment."

A longtime social activist, Sandra works for a Texas labor union. She is sixty years old, but youthful and vivacious; only a few lines on her face hint at her age. Her eyes sparkle, her black hair shines, and she gestures enthusiastically with her hands. She wears boots over slim-fitting pants and two sweaters—it's a chilly desert night in January. Even though her first language is English, Sandra speaks with me in Spanish.

A few minutes later Carlos walks over with a firm step and joins us. His appearance catches me off guard. I have seen him before in photos and videos, with a robust frame, deep voice, and impassioned way of speaking that lent him an imposing air. The Carlos in front of me has the same wavy sandy hair, pale complexion, strong nose, mustache, sideburns, and somewhat uneven beard, but is someone else: thirty pounds lighter, the skin on his face hanging slack around squinty eyes, his voice raspy, tired. Sandra tells me that her husband was diagnosed with cancer of the larynx a few months before. He is recovering from an aggressive course of radiation treatment.

Carlos asks for a glass of water without ice and starts to talk, gesturing with his hands for emphasis. He's an effective orator: like a preacher, but without the arrogance. He smiles and speaks with passion. In recent months, all of his time and energy have been consumed by a particular kind of case: Mexicans living in exile in the United States because of violence in their home country.

"Everything is political," Carlos tells me the day we meet. "It has to be political to make the case for someone applying for asylum, to make the U.S. government understand what is happening." When the Reyes family's case found its way to Carlos, he began to see a pattern in the stories of his clients—journalists and social justice and human rights activists and defenders—and their motivations for fleeing to the United States. He began studying "those individuals who, before the attack, had been working on protecting democracy." A human rights defender, he says, is someone who works professionally in the defense of human rights, while an activist (e.g., a family member of the disappeared) seeks justice where the state fails to provide it. Within just a few months, Carlos had compiled a list of twenty-one human rights defenders who had been assassinated. Justice had not been served in a single case.

The asylum cases coming from Guadalupe are, for Carlos, personal. Born in 1954 in El Paso, he describes himself as a "pocho"—a slang word roughly translating to "Americanized Mexican"—but strongly identifies with Mexico. His mother was from Guadalupe; his grandfather was mayor of the city. As in all border communities, Carlos's family home "on the other side" was an extension of his own.

"We knew through our family that things were really bad, that Chapo Guzmán had gotten there in 2008, and they were killing the leaders of La Linea," Carlos explains, referring to the local cartel in Juárez. Some of Carlos's relatives were among that group—"a little bit removed"—so they knew the details. Then the Reyes Salazar family was referred to him.

The family's case, Carlos says, represents the entire system of "authorized crime" in Mexico. "The criminals don't function without authorization from the state," he says, "whether it's on a municipal, state, or federal level." When criminal groups first arrive in a town, they tend to identify and target the area's political leadership first as a form of "ideological cleansing," Carlos explains. Over the course of several election cycles for governor of the state of Chihuahua, Guadalupe was the only place in the entire state where a leftist candidate from the PRD party won. The candidates who prevailed there were from the Reyeses' party; the family was therefore considered "dangerous."

Aside from relying on open, obvious repression and

expelling its people, Mexico also considers those who seek asylum in the United States to be traitors. "People who are under attack are expected to stay there and fight to the death to defend the country that is pushing them out," he says.

We are having coffee after dinner, and Carlos gestures forcefully with his hands to compensate for the weakness of his voice. He finds it troubling that since the Institutional Revolutionary Party (PRI), which governed Mexico for seventy years before losing in 2000, came back into power in 2012 under President Enrique Peña Nieto, the government publicly maintains that everything is just fine in Mexico. The United States has bought the story without question. The media have picked up the message and broadcast it repeatedly, and the narrative has swayed international opinion.[1]

"People applying for asylum in the United States are having their petitions denied, even though extortion and death threats are still happening there, in the streets, in everyday life," Carlos recounts, heatedly. "The U.S. authorities aren't asking why people come here without papers . . . The reason they came here is fear, to escape extortion."

We're about to leave the restaurant, but Carlos pauses to tell me a joke he heard from some men being held in immigration detention: "A Honduran, Salvadoran, Mexican, and Guatemalan are in a van. Who's driving?" He waits a beat. "Immigration!" He delivers the punch line with a raucous laugh.

Martín Huéramo is nervous. He strides assuredly into Carlos Spector's law office, but then looks around anxiously for a place to sit. He wrings his hands and shifts impatiently in his seat. In a few days he will appear before a judge who will review his case for asylum. His children's future and his own will depend on the evidence and testimony that he, Carlos, and others present.

Carlos is tough on Martín as they talk about his case, and focuses on the political aspect of his argument. They sit side by side behind Carlos's mahogany desk, a statuette of Lady Justice, balance in hand, watching over them. They go over the weak points in his defense, which could jeopardize his asylum case. Carlos demands his client's complete concentration, and asks him for some documentation. One by one, these cold, impersonal appearances before a judge decide the fate of the exiled.

Even before he was a lawyer, Carlos already thought in the political language he has mastered so well. By the time he enrolled in law school at thirty years old, he had already earned a master's degree in sociology and held several jobs with organizations involved with the Central American and Mexican communities. It was the eighties, and amnesty for millions of undocumented immigrants would soon be passed into law. Also around this time, Carlos met Sandra Garza, now his wife.

Sandra's family traces its roots back to a time in South Texas "before Mexico was Mexico, when it was a Spanish territory," as she likes to point out. Sandra was involved in the pro-immigrant movement spearheaded by Humberto "Bert" Corona, the Chicano activist who led movements in support of labor unions and rights for undocumented immigrants—a stance which would eventually cause a rift between him and his longtime ally, the farmworker activist Cesar Chavez. During these formative years, Sandra also worked with students who fled Mexico in the wake of the student massacre of 1968, and another violent attack on students in 1971 in an incident known as "el halconazo."

"I met Sandra when she was an organizer for the Ladies' Garment Workers' Union here in El Paso," Carlos recalls with a smile. A year has passed since our conversation over dinner at the Mexican restaurant, and now we're meeting again in his office, in a building on a corner in a popular El Paso neighborhood. Carlos is a new man: although still lean, he's put on weight, his hair has grown back, his beard has filled in, his gaze is sharp, his voice strong once again.

"Some friends told me, you've got to meet this girl, she's doing what you're doing," he says. "When I was introduced to her, I saw she was involved with the same things. I had met the woman who would accompany me, sometimes follow me, and sometimes lead me in the social struggle that comes at such a high emotional and political cost."

For the Spectors, that struggle has become a way of life. The first political asylum case Carlos won was in 1991. The petitioner, Ernesto Poblano, was a candidate for Mexico's conservative National Action Party (PAN), opposing PRI. The mayor of Ojinaga, a town in the state of Chihuahua, Poblano received a message one day stating "that he would not be allowed to win and govern," Carlos explains. Poblano fled across the border, Carlos successfully demonstrated that his client had been persecuted, and he won the asylum case. That was followed by cases representing other political leaders from PAN or the leftist Revolutionary Democratic Party (PRD), dissidents from PRI, and labor leaders.

The political landscape since the nineties, however, "has changed a great deal," he says, because of "massive, large-scale repression. In the eighties and nineties," he explains, "the repression was clearly aimed at leaders." But even when, during the presidency of Carlos Salinas, more people began to flee and more leftists were assassinated, "Mexicans weren't applying for political asylum. If it's rare for this kind of violence to be acknowledged now, just imagine back then."

Originally established as a relief measure by the United Nations in 1952, political asylum allows people suffering from persecution to seek refuge in a country other than their own if they can demonstrate that the persecution falls under one or more of five categories: religion, race, national minority status, political opinion, or membership in a social group. The persecution can be carried out by the state or by a particular group from which the state is either unwilling or unable to provide protection for the individual. Political asylum grew out of an accord between nations following World War II, at a time when fascism and Communism were considered the main sources of persecution.

"The law has not evolved along with the social, political, and economic changes of today," Carlos says. It fails to comprehend the reality of a "failed state" that persecutes Mexican citizens, he says, which "is partly why political asylum is denied to Mexicans."

Historically, political asylum has been used as a tool to punish the enemies and reward the friends of the nation where asylum seekers apply. For immigration lawyers, the clearest example is Cuba. Because Cuba is ruled by a Communist regime politically opposed to the United States, the U.S. consequently welcomed Cuban immigrants with open arms (until January 2017, when President Barack Obama announced an end to the policy known as "wet foot, dry foot"). "People fleeing persecution in Communist countries or Eastern Europe," says Carlos, receive a far warmer welcome in the United States "than those trying to escape persecution in countries that are viewed as 'friends' of the United States, like Mexico, El Salvador, Honduras, Colombia, and Argentina."

In 1980 the United States Refugee Act officially recognized the right to petition for asylum just as civil wars were breaking out in Central America. Carlos believes these factors created what he calls "the country's political conscience": the view in the United States that only a civil war or a national tragedy justified an individual seeking asylum. This meant that most cases from Mexicans were denied.

Despite this, the number of asylum seekers from Mexico began to creep up during Salinas de Gortari's presidential administration (1988 to 1994). Salinas came into office after a bitter campaign battle against his leftist rival, Cuauhtémoc Cárdenas, colored by widespread suspicion of electoral fraud on the part of the PRI, the governing party. The most radical leftist leaders were persecuted, and in some cases assassinated, in several states across Mexico during Salinas's presidency.

Soon, cases of people exiled because of Salinas de Gortari reached Carlos's office. In response, he crafted a strategy based on cases of exile in other Central American countries, as well as the Chileans exiled from Augusto Pinochet's dictatorship in the sixties. Attacks at the time were focused on leaders with very specific characteristics and in particular circumstances. Since power was centralized, repression was also centralized and channeled to a direct object.

Repression and persecution in Mexico have changed since

the PRI's fall from power in 2000: the PAN, the rightist party, now dominates the federal government, and many municipalities are in the hands of the leftist PRD. With power decentralized among three political parties, violence extends indiscriminately, with few limits and concrete objectives. Most cases of persecution originate in small cities and towns, rather than Mexico's major cities—in areas key to narcotrafficking, near to oil wells or with access to water. Cartels, in league with the state, can provide, or deny, access to these areas.

"It's often difficult to make the case for asylum based on political views," Carlos explains, "but when you're a candidate for office, when you're a writer or someone who's constantly criticizing the government publicly, it's much easier." When President Felipe Calderón's war on drug trafficking prompted an exodus, for example, Carlos's strongest asylum cases were journalists. It was relatively easy to demonstrate persecution based on political beliefs or on their membership in a social group—in this case, the journalism profession.

Carlos began to take on more cases from journalists and human rights defenders, the vast majority from the state of Chihuahua, and became an expert in this new condition of exile-asylum from Mexico to the United States. Carlos, Sandra, their daughter Alejandra, and a few other people in their office began taking on these cases pro bono or for a nominal fee. When the Reyes case came to the Spectors, the evidence of massive repression was clear. Such cases were easy because they embodied the very definition of political asylum. Considered symbolic cases, they could be used to educate people on their options within the immigration system.

Carlos started to win some cases through the political asylum office, which is very different from having to go before a judge. There are two political asylum categories: affirmative asylum and defensive asylum. Those who enter the United States legally, with a visa or work permit, can go to one of the asylum offices throughout the country to apply for affirmative asylum. The process is more friendly, and the staff interviewing candidates for asylum there specialize in the subject; they are more sensitive to applicants' circumstances and can process cases more accurately. Those who apply for asylum at border crossings or those detained while attempting to cross the border illegally are applying for defensive asylum; they try to defend themselves against deportation, presenting an argument for their asylum petition. Their first contact is with immigration agents, who generally do not have the training or knowledge to deal with victims of violence. The standard procedure is to arrest the asylum applicant, then schedule a court date for them to go before a judge. And that is where the battle begins.

"I never thought we would have to appeal these cases in court," Carlos remarks, still incredulous that asylum is routinely denied to victims of well-documented, clear cases of violence like the Reyes family. "That's when I realized the Mexican government is not satisfied with the U.S. rejecting 98 percent of applications. They want them to deny 100 percent of the cases." He recalls cases in which the Inter-American Court of Human Rights or the state and federal commissions on human rights intervened on behalf of migrants accused of transgressions such as criticizing the government or the army. Those cases have been rejected.

It was time to depart from the strategy that had worked with Central American exiles in the eighties, Carlos decided. If that wave of exiles had been characterized by invisibility, people coming from Mexico would have to be highly visible, making public declarations and denunciations and criticizing the Mexican state. "Because the problem is binational," Carlos argues, "the solution has to be binational: attacking and criticizing the source of the problem from here." The United States is as culpable as Mexico, not only denying petitions but openly discouraging petitioners by insulting and detaining immigrants at border crossings. Such rejections in turn discourage lawyers from taking on strong cases due to low rates of success, Carlos says.

Winning political asylum cases for Mexicans has not been profitable for the Spectors, but it has increased the firm's profile. They currently handle a caseload of 250 clients, including a hundred families, and one by one, the cases are being approved. Carlos has won cases for six members of the Reyes family, for instance, including Saúl and Sara. This is an extraordinary feat, considering the national statistics: of every hundred cases of Mexicans applying for asylum, ninety-eight are denied.

Although the figures are discouraging, asylum seekers keep coming. According to the U.S. Department of Justice, of 3,650 asylum applications presented by Mexicans in 2008, only 73 were granted. By 2011, the number of applicants had doubled, but of 7,616 applications, only 107 were granted. In fiscal year 2013, the applications reached 10,177, and of those, 155 were approved; by 2015 the number of applications dropped to 8,923, and 203 were approved. This represents a sea change from 2006, before Felipe Calderón's war on narcotrafficking began, when 133 applications were filed.[2]

On top of enduring a complicated, challenging process, applicants and their lawyers must contend with the far right in both countries; those in the United States argue that asylum seekers are doing so to obtain green cards, while their Mexican counterparts refer to asylum seekers as "busca-papeles" ("looking for papers"), traitors, or criminals. And the Mexican government, Carlos says, consistently echoes this rhetoric.

Carlos tells me Marisol Valles's story as an example. For months, Marisol was known as "the bravest woman in Mexico," a nickname initially coined by the Spanish daily *El País* and picked up by the other media outlets following her story. A twenty-year-old college student studying criminology, Marisol became the chief of police in Práxedis G. Guerrero, a town in the Juárez Valley in Chihuahua, where her predecessors had met one of two fates: they were assassinated or fled after receiving death threats from narcotraffickers. Marisol took a job that no one else wanted, with the promise that she would head a police corps of mostly female officers, avoid direct confrontations with criminal gangs, and focus on devising policies to prevent violence and crime on the local level.

Four months later, Marisol began receiving the usual threats. She chose to leave the country, turning herself in to an immigration agent and applying for asylum.[3] Her husband, her parents, her two sisters, and her infant son were with her, with nothing more than the clothes on their backs and their birth certificates. After spending a few days in a U.S. immigration detention center, they were released to live with relatives, ten people in one house. Eight months later, they still had not been granted permission to work, which was usually granted to applicants while their asylum cases are wending their way through the courts.

When questioned by the media about Marisol's departure, the mayor's office in Práxedis Guerrero denied that she had received any threats, asserting that she had asked to take a week off for personal reasons and that she would be fired if she did not return to work. The governor of Chihuahua, César Duarte, went further, accusing Marisol of exploiting her "fame" to move to the United States, thereby damaging Chihuahua's image, and insinuating that she had left her job due to romantic problems. Then Carlos Spector took her case.

That the morals of people leaving their country to stay alive are questioned infuriates Carlos. He maintains that government authorities seeking to protect their reputation are as guilty of this practice as the news media. After Marisol's departure, for example, "an article was published saying she had been planning to come to the United States ever since she was a little girl, because she wore Polo T-shirts when she was seven or eight." He smiles wryly, shaking his head. "I'm proud to have such far-sighted clients." Even some human rights groups, he says, "view people who apply for political asylum as abandoning the fight for Mexico. Maybe they would rather see them die in Mexico. To them, that is a good Mexican: someone who gives their life, not someone who tries to save it through political asylum." Marisol's case was eventually closed: she obtained a work permit but was not granted political asylum.

After deciding to focus on asylum cases, the Spector family established the organization Mexicans in Exile for Mexicans arriving in the El Paso area, fleeing violence in Chihuahua and bringing their cases to Carlos's law practice. The group's goal is not just to win asylum but also to denounce the violence in Mexico, to provide guidance and support to those fleeing the country, and to demand justice from the Mexican authorities for all of the unsolved murders and disappearances. Just as the organization was getting off the ground in 2012, Carlos was dealt a tremendous blow: he was diagnosed with cancer of the throat and tongue and nearly died.

"I couldn't talk or eat," Carlos recalls. "Either someone wanted to shut me up, or to send me a message . . . I got the chance to taste death, through chemotherapy and radiation . . . I realized life is very short, and you have to do something that fills your soul . . . I didn't go to law school so I could make a lot of money; I went to make justice. And when I was so sick, Carlos Gutiérrez came to me—his legs had been cut off—telling me, 'You can do it.' And Saúl Reyes, whose brothers had been killed, telling me, 'Don't give up.' They helped me to see that we are making a difference. They are saving our souls."

# 3

## Constructing a Border

On February 2, 2007, a group of about fifty people in fifteen cars, led by the San Diego–based pro-immigrant organization Border Angels (Angeles de la Frontera), gathered in San Ysidro, California, at the westernmost point of the U.S.-Mexico border. A fence made of rectangular bars spaced just far enough apart for an arm to pass through separated the two countries. Now, those spaces between the bars are covered with metallic mesh that barely allows a finger to pass through. This site is popularly known as "la esquina de Latinoamérica," or "the corner of Latin America": the northernmost point along the continent that those of us growing up in Mexico and all points south of it were taught to call ours.

The group was about to start the Migrant March, a two-week trip making stops at the main border cities in both the United States and Mexico, ending in Brownsville, Texas, at the easternmost point on the border. The goal was to gather stories from people who lived on one side of the line or the other, talking about how immigration reform could benefit them and how a wall between the two countries would affect their daily lives. A few months earlier, the numerous pro-immigrant marches of 2006 had put the immigration issue back in the political spotlight. As a result, in 2007 Congress was debating a legislative initiative that would permit the construction of a contiguous wall running along the entire length of the U.S.-Mexico border.[1]

The imaginary line that begins at the Pacific Ocean runs for 3,326 kilometers, or 1,989 miles—according to the Treaty of Guadalupe Hidalgo, signed by the two countries in 1848—and ends where the Río Grande empties into the Gulf of Mexico. Passing through water, over mountains, and through the desert, and often marked by sections of cement wall topped with razor wire (remnants of different moments in history), the border is a long, meandering scar tarnishing landscapes, forests, and neighboring communities that have never been divided in practice. One could stop anywhere along the border and see that on both sides, the water does not change color, the dry land gives rise to the same dust, the wind sweeps from one side to the other, seeping through the bars, drifting back again. The longer one travels along it, the more senseless the imaginary line becomes.

As we know, hundreds of thousands of undocumented immigrants come through the border every year, as well as 350,000 people who cross legally. One way or the other, this line has the power to erase or recreate one's identity. Tell me how, why, when, where, and in which direction you crossed the line, and I will tell you who you are.

The group participating in the Migrant March chose February 2 to begin their journey: the day of the celebration of the Virgin of Candelaria in Mexico. It is also the anniversary of the signing of the Treaty of Guadalupe Hidalgo, which marked the end of the Mexican-American War (1846 to 1848). With the signing of the treaty, Mexico ceded to the United States territory that included present-day California, Arizona, Nevada, and Utah, and parts of Colorado, New Mexico, and Wyoming.

The treaty established arbitrary dividing lines between California and Baja California, Sonora and Arizona, New Mexico and western Chihuahua. It was decided that the Río Grande would serve as the border between Texas and the Mexican states of Coahuila, Nuevo León, and eastern Chihuahua. Areas like Paso del Norte, which for centuries had served as an intermediary point, providing protection, rest, and supplies to travelers heading north to New Mexico or south to Chihuahua, Zacatecas, or Mexico City, suddenly became border towns.

But the border between Mexico and the United States is more than just a line on a map, and its construction did not begin with the signing of a treaty. It is the product of a long chain of actions and complex relationships affected by political, cultural, racial, economic, military, and security interests, and by the dynamics of social groups living on both sides. The border is a laboratory that legitimizes and excludes; one side defines the other, reaffirming and reinforcing differences.

Historian Carlos González Herrera has studied the phenomenon of the border's construction more than perhaps anyone else. In his book *La frontera que vino del norte*, the author explains how, during the late nineteenth and early twentieth centuries, the geopolitical dividing lines between the United States and Mexico were established as the binational relationship between the two developed, designating people as "legal" or "alien." Herrera starts his analysis in the El Paso–Juárez border region.

Like other old cities in the southwestern United States, the area around what is now known as Juárez–El Paso was named in reference to a geographic point, and in honor of a Catholic figure. Nuestra Señora de Guadalupe de los Mansos de El Paso del Río del Norte was established in 1659 as a Franciscan mission. It was known informally as Paso del Norte, and it became the primary access point to New Mexico, a jurisdiction on which it was dependent until 1823, when the area was added to the state of Chihuahua. In 1824, the Congress of that Mexican state made the name Paso del Norte official.

Because of its strategic location, the region—and, in particular, the Santa Fe trail in New Mexico—was key to commercial trade between the cities of Chihuahua and San Luis Missouri. El Paso de Norte sits exactly at the point where the states of New Mexico and Texas meet on the Mexican border. This factor compelled a group of foreign merchants to settle in the region on the northern shores of the Río Bravo, which after the Treaty of Guadalupe Hidalgo would fall into the hands of the United States.

Shortly thereafter, the county of El Paso was formed in Texas. The settlement to the north of the border was called Franklin, while the area on the Mexican side was still known as Paso del Norte, until September 16, 1888, when it was renamed Ciudad Juárez in memory of President Benito Juárez, who had been forced temporarily by the invasion of

French troops to relocate the seat of government there between 1865 and 1866. Franklin, which was home to a powerful, striving Anglo-American elite, then changed its name to El Paso.

In the coming years, the border area, with El Paso on the U.S. side and Juárez in Mexico, took on a practical character. It was a place of exile for dissidents, of whom the brothers Ricardo and Enrique Flores Magón were perhaps the most well-known, protesting dictator Porfirio Díaz's regime from 1876 to 1911. It was a natural arms market before, during, and after the Mexican Revolution, which began in 1910. Aside from creating a rupture in relations between the United States and Mexico, that conflict generated a U.S. concept of the border charged with classism and racism. Militarization after 1915 brought increased alcohol consumption and prostitution to the zone, and the region became synonymous with immorality and disease in the collective imagination. For the rest of the decade and into the 1920s, the city could not establish security and stability.

The border between Mexico and the United States as we know it today began to take shape at a time when both countries were going through critical, defining stages. Once internal U.S. cohesion was consolidated, the nation began to test the limits and reach of its transnational power. For its part, Mexico constructed a post-revolutionary identity with Mexico City as its epicenter, some 1,100 miles to the south of El Paso–Juárez. Even though several leaders of the new regime were originally from the northern Mexican states (Chihuahua, Coahuila, and Sonora), the border area was rugged, desolate terrain that functioned more as a distancing buffer than a link.

Paso del Norte became a testing ground for the border's identity and its broad implications. There began to be a differentiation of conduct and popular culture "to make it clear to Mexicans on both sides that this point was a haven for civilization and Western democracy," writes González Herrera, "which they clearly were not a part of." He emphasizes that "the legal framework, international treaties, and the body of regulations that the United States established to distinguish the alien-other-foreigner" were in no way "internalized within the consciousness of actual citizens on the ground."

The professor's description reminded me of an episode that took place on the El Paso–Juárez border around the time of the Migrant March, shortly before a conversation I had with John Cook, mayor of El Paso from 2005 to 2013. In February 2007, when Mexican president Felipe Calderón had recently assumed office and no one could yet foresee the consequences of his war on narcotrafficking, Cook—who before being the mayor had been a professor, a businessman, an army intelligence agent, and a city councilman—led a group of twelve mayors of border cities in Texas and Mexico to Washington, D.C., to meet with legislators and Secretary of National Security Michael Chertoff, express their opposition to the border wall construction project, and explore alternative solutions. Cook's motto at the time: "If the federal government has money to build a wall, give it to me and I'll build a bridge."

"We told them we didn't want a wall in Texas because our main business partner is Mexico," explained Cook. He had surprised me with his openness and willingness to meet even though I did not have an appointment. I showed up at his office, told a security guard the reason for my visit, and ten minutes later, I was talking to the mayor in his office. At that time, before Joint Operation Chihuahua would wreak havoc in Juárez, the mayor said that for every ten jobs generated in the manufacturing industry on the Mexican side, one more job was created in El Paso. "There could be a devaluation of the dollar, and it will take months to be felt in El Paso," he pointed out. "But when the peso is devalued, we feel it the same day."

Two months earlier, the mayors of Del Río, Texas, and Cuidad Acuña, Coahuila, had taken a trip to Eagle Pass to meet with the mayor of that city on the U.S. side, and the mayor of Pedras Negras on the Mexican side. The message was clear: Our communities are sisters. They can't put a wall between us.

"Our community is very pro-immigrant, so what we need is a reform that resolves immigration problems, so workers can come in legally," Cook told me before I left his office. "There's no reason to have a father living on the other side of the border who can't see his children on this side. That is not humanitarian, and it's not what our country is about."

The day after my meeting with the mayor, I crossed the border south into Juárez in the morning. That day, on Paso del Norte, one of the bridges that spans the cities, what we had discussed was on clear display: people rushing this way and that; people from one side blending with people from the other. When I was halfway across the bridge, a man walked right up to me, smiled, and said, "You're the journalist from California, right?" Even though he was not wearing his uniform, I recognized him as the security guard who had let me into Mayor Cook's office. He was a cheerful *juarense*, a Juárez native, who crossed the bridge every day to go to work in El Paso's mayoral office.

The construction of the border with Mexico followed two guiding principles that dominated the overall vision of bilateral relations in the United States at the turn of the century. The first principle defined the country to the south as a source of cheap, unskilled labor that could be easily expelled because of Mexico's geographic proximity. The second principle characterized Mexicans as permanent strangers. This served, among other things, to reinforce Americans' self-perception. These principles allowed a system that vigilantly tracked the movement of people from south to north to emerge along the border. To this day they are registered, classified, and labeled according to a hierarchy of values in order to be controlled.

This control, rather than preventing Mexicans from crossing into the United States, was the original, primary objective of the border in its early days. The practices of observing, asking, touching, and, in the case of some immigrants and workers (e.g., the members of the Braceros Program, seasonal farm workers "imported" from Mexico), bathing, disinfecting, and vaccinating began to form part of a series of increasingly restrictive, intrusive, and violent protocols.

The border, which registered the entry and geographic location of the thousands of workers arriving in the southwestern United States, hardened after Congress passed the Immigration Act in 1917. With regulations in hand, the Immigration Service was armed with the legal justification to classify Mexicans as foreigners who could be subjected to numerous obstacles to freely crossing the border, including an eight-dollar tax imposed on any foreigner entering the country. This was followed by the bureaucratization of border control: by 1923, 300 employees were dispatched to border crossing points from Tijuana to Brownsville. In 1924, the border patrol was officially formed; by 1940, it had 1,500 agents. This number continued to rise in the decades that followed, reaching 20,000 agents by 2014.[2] Today, land border crossings are equipped with technology that can scan an entire car, with the passengers still inside. The passport card, the size of a credit card, contains a chip which allows it to be read by a scanner several yards away, before the traveler even reaches the checkpoint. And in an unspoken agreement, everyone knows that the words "gun" or "bomb" must never be uttered anywhere near a border checkpoint, or at customs inspection or in an airport, because the authorities are always listening.

In spite of everything, people inhabiting this extensive region over the centuries, including a significant population of Mexican or Hispanic descent, have not been able to cut ties completely according to strict international boundaries. Border areas are accustomed to a stream of constant communication and mobility, where daily life has gone on for decades far away from the governments headquartered in Washington, D.C., and Mexico City. Communities on both sides of the line have remained connected by tradition, family and personal ties, and strong economic interests.

Another scene from the Migrant March of 2007 illustrates this concept well. At one of the less-traveled border crossings, where Del Río, Texas, meets Ciudad Acuña, Coahuila, around eighty people gathered to greet the marchers. Sitting around tables at a Mexican restaurant on the U.S. side, under a sign that read, "Welcome to our Del Río–Acuña Community," the group talked about the two cities as if they were one, as if they were not divided by a river marking a border, where the U.S. government planned to construct a wall. "That's like building a wall right through a house, with one family living in it," explained Jay Johnson, an activist and founder of the Border Ambassadors project, and Del Río resident.

Small towns on both sides have been friends, neighbors, and brothers and sisters for centuries. There is nothing to indicate the difference between one country and the other. Before the terrorist attacks of September 11, 2001, people routinely went back and forth across the border.

But with the changes in border security measures, the reality for people on the border has become absurd. At the exclusive Lajitas golf resort in Texas, an expensive destination, virtually all of the workers come from small towns in Mexico—like the security officer working in the mayor's office in El Paso. On the U.S. side, there are no towns for miles around the resort, so the relationship benefits both Mexico, which lacks jobs, and the United States, which lacks labor. But after regulations were changed, people living in Mexico were only allowed to cross into the United States at official gates, and the closest official border gate for these workers was two hours away. Of course, the workers continued, illegally, to cross over where they always had. In a symbolic protest, the owner of the resort installed a hole on his golf course in Mexican territory.

The day after Del Río, the Migrant March reached Laredo, Texas, just as the city prepared for its most important celebration of the year: February 17, George Washington's birthday. The day's festivities would culminate in a special ceremony known as Abrazo, or "hug." The ritual is as simple and beautiful as its name suggests: residents of both sides of the border, Laredo in the United States and Nuevo Laredo in Mexico, walk over the bridge that joins the two cities, and, at the midpoint, exchange hugs to express their friendship.

"Local authorities, senators, deputies, lots of people come from the other side, and practically the whole city goes from this side," explains Juan Ramírez, vice mayor of Laredo. "A little boy and girl from Mexico dressed in traditional Mexican clothing lead their group, and the same on this side, a little boy and girl in traditional Texas clothing."

This ritual of friendship renewal has been celebrated at the border crossing for 119 years. There were plans to build a wall there, too.

# Part Two
# Exile and Asylum

# 4

# Annunciation House

## The Asylum Tradition

A red brick building sits on the corner ten blocks from the border between Mexico and the United States. Erected almost a century ago, it's in El Paso, Texas. Juárez, Mexico, is just across the river. And everyone knows that even though the two cities are only steps apart, those from the other side of the border who find their way to that red brick building can finally feel safe.

Since its founding in 1978, Annunciation House has offered shelter, a bed, a shower, and a hot meal to the homeless and anyone with nowhere else to go. The concept first took hold in 1976, when a group of young Catholic idealists got together in El Paso, searching for a meaningful mission for themselves, and proposed the idea of creating a space to serve people without a home. In 1978, the Catholic archdiocese in El Paso decided that the project was worthwhile and gave them the second floor of the brick building to use, on the condition that they also maintain it. And with that, Annunciation House was born.

Rubén García was among that group of young Catholics. As director of the Office for Young Adults at the diocese, he decided to focus all of his enthusiasm and energy on the new project. He and four others moved into the second floor and began seeking out "the poorest of the poor" to lend a helping hand.

"When the House first opened, there were only two other shelters in El Paso," recalls Rubén, who is still the director of Annunciation House. "At the time, we didn't know those shelters did not accept undocumented people." It was 1978, and after the end of the Bracero Program, which between 1942 and 1964 had allowed Mexican workers to enter the United States on a temporary basis, immigration laws had hardened. No social service organization could offer aid to anyone who was undocumented.

"We found out when we were flooded with immigrants who told us they had looked for help and had been refused 'because we don't have papers,'" Rubén remembers. "We understood then that immigrants were the most vulnerable group. They were the poorest of the poor."

Ever since the first opponents of Mexican dictator Porfirio Díaz's regime made El Paso the headquarters for their conspiratorial operations over a century ago, the El Paso/Juárez area has been the setting for border crossings related to asylum and exile from Mexico and sometimes even from Central America. "The house was founded in 1978, right when the Sandinistas defeated Somoza in Nicaragua and took control of the country," Rubén remembers. "That's when the guerrillas in El Salvador and Guatemala rose up, hoping they could overthrow their governments too, which as we know did not happen. But the civil wars caused a wave of exiled migrants, and El Paso was one of the border towns where they landed. So we took them in at the House."

With increased border security efforts and a hardening of immigration politics in the wake of the terrorist attacks of September 11, 2001, undocumented immigration into the United States has grown increasingly dangerous but has not diminished. Over the past two decades, Annunciation House has remained full, sheltering between 100 and 125 people on average. Since they first opened their doors, Rubén estimates that he and his volunteer staff have welcomed about 125,000 people.

Saúl Reyes crossed the Santa Fe bridge with his wife and their three children in February 2011. When the Reyes family arrived in El Paso, the first place to shelter them was Annunciation House.

Dozens of families have stories like that of the Reyes family. They have been harassed, persecuted, and physically attacked, their property has been ransacked or burned to the ground, and their attackers enjoy full impunity. One study by the Autonomous University of Chihuahua found that since 2008, when violence in the area escalated, approximately 100,000 Mexicans have moved from Juárez to somewhere in the United States; half of those moved to El Paso.[1]

Similar to the wave of upper-class pro-Díaz Mexicans at the beginning of the twentieth century, some leaving Juárez have the resources, a visa, or a work permit allowing them to stay in the United States legally. Others, like the Reyes family, thought they had a strong enough case to win asylum and decided to embark on the legal process. But these cases are the exception. Although migration and asylum are commonplace in El Paso del Norte, U.S. legislation is restrictive when it comes to granting political asylum to citizens of countries like Mexico, El Salvador, Guatemala, and Honduras. Given that asylum laws date from the 1980s and were formulated based on the geopolitics of the Cold War, those who come from Mexico and Central America are not considered eligible for protection since their governments are, at least theoretically, democracies. Immigrants from countries like China, Iran, or Venezuela, which the United States defines as non-democratic, have approval rates for asylum applications of between 70 and 82 percent, while the rates of approval for asylum petitions from Honduras and Guatemala are around 15 to 16 percent. Petitions from El Salvador are approved less than 8 percent of the time, and approval rates for Mexico are barely 2 percent. Faced with these dim prospects, the majority choose the only option they have: entering the country without documentation or with a temporary visa that will soon lapse, and fading into anonymity among the 11.5 million undocumented people living in the country.

Father Arturo Bañuelas knows his city well. The priest of the San Pio parish for twenty-six years, he recently moved to a new parish also in El Paso and has been closely involved with Rubén's work at Annunciation House. The shelter's operation is indispensable, he asserts, especially with all the exiles from the recent violence in Juárez. That city and El Paso, Father Arturo points out, are bound by "very strong economic, cultural, and religious ties. The people here are one community. Now we understand that after the violence broke out, for each person killed [in Juárez], a hundred more on both sides of the border have been affected . . . We are closer to each other here than to the capitals of our own countries. So the people who had the resources found a way to get out when the violence started. The ones who stayed in Juárez are the poorest, the ones who could not pay for their escape."

One morning in July 2014, Rubén got a phone call. It was an agent from Immigration and Customs Enforcement (ICE). The agent told him about the growing numbers of underage migrants traveling across the border alone, or with their mothers, then detained around the Río Grande in South Texas. Immigration authorities could only process them, but once they were released on bond, they had nowhere to go and had no family or host to receive them. The ICE agent told Rubén that planes were about to fly into El Paso with 140 migrants. They would be released under their own recognizance. For the ones with nowhere to go, the agent asked, could Rubén take them in?

Although Rubén was used to taking in entire families, the phone call surprised him. For years, Annunciation House had been subjected to raids and harrassment by the border patrol and ICE agents. Gradually, however, the harassment had abated, to the point where ICE agents themselves escorted undocumented pregnant women, sick people, and children to Annunciation House. And the house had provided temporary shelter to approximately 2,500 undocumented minors from Central America during the 2014 surge.

Annunciation House has become an icon for El Paso, a community that boasts of being the "Ellis Island of the southeastern U.S.," according to Mexican American journalist Alfredo Corchado, whose family, originally from Durango, made El Paso their home after spending a few years in the fields in California.

"This city is home to people who want to reinvent themselves, who are fleeing hard times and need security, a way to start over," Alfredo says, a hint of pride in his voice. "It's a city that takes in the oppressed, the dispossessed, people who have lived through bloodshed and uncertainty."

In May 1976, while he was still working for the archdiocese, Rubén invited Mother Teresa to visit his group of young adults. She accepted the invitation, and a relationship grew between them. Two years later she asked Rubén to work on a project she was starting. But Rubén had just received permission from the archdiocese to create a shelter for the poor, and he told her he could not accept her invitation. Mother Teresa responded in a letter praising his decision: "Now you can go forth and do a work of annunciation. You will announce the good news and give people a home in the name of Jesus."

From then on, Annunciation House's destiny was settled.

# 5

# Political Asylum

Sheltering Arms, but Not for Everyone

Rocío Hernández has twice been held in immigration detention in the United States. Both times, in October 2013 and March 2014, she had come from Mexico to request political asylum at the border crossing. And both times, after spending a month in detention, she was deported. When she first asked for asylum, she had been living in Mexico, her birth country, for four years. Before that, she had spent fifteen years living undocumented in the United States.

"I had gone back to Mexico to go to school, for the chance to have a professional career," she told me over the phone in 2014. She was in Veracruz, where she had gone to live after being deported for the second time.

With long black hair, a dark complexion, bright eyes, and a wide, vivacious smile, Rocío migrated to the United States with her family, without papers, when she was four years old. Her life unfolded like that of a typical American girl: she went to school and thought about what she would do when she grew up. But when she tried to continue her education after high school, the door slammed shut. She did not have a social security number.

"At the time I wanted to go to art school, which costs twice as much as a regular school, and I couldn't get a scholarship, or financial aid for immigrants," Rocío recalls. "My parents did not have a good financial situation. We couldn't apply for a loan."

So when Rocío was nineteen, she decided to return to Mexico and continue her education there, leaving behind High Point, North Carolina, her parents, her seventeen-year-old sister, and her thirteen-year-old brother. She went to the Mexican state of Veracruz, where her family was from, and enrolled in a program for graphic design and public relations. The experience was harder than she had imagined. She felt like a foreigner in the country she had considered her own. And the state her parents fondly remembered had become one of the most dangerous in Mexico, where drug cartels and organized crime operated with impunity, journalists were assassinated, and young people were kidnapped, their bodies discovered weeks later in mass graves. But in spite of the abundant evidence of the violence in Veracruz, the evidence presented by Rocío on her particular situation, and the fact that she had lived most of her life in the United States and her entire family was there, her case was not considered strong enough for an asylum petition.

"My dream was to live in Los Angeles someday and work in a fashion design company, but I couldn't," she tells me as we finish our conversation. "The truth is I don't see myself living in Mexico, I'm afraid here. So I'm considering going to London to study art, or fashion." It has been five years since she last saw her parents; they cannot travel to Mexico because of their immigration status.

Most of the 1.5 million undocumented immigrants living in the United States have been an integral part of its society, economy, and culture for much longer than one or two years. Only 14 percent of undocumented immigrants have been in the country for less than five years, while 66 percent have made their home in the United States for a decade or more.[1] Just like Rocío, most have deep roots in the United States through their communities and families. But the law still defines them as "aliens," and they are denied the opportunity to work, to pursue higher education, and to build a stable life. The proportion of long-term residents is even higher among the 6 million undocumented immigrants from Mexico;[2] just 7 percent of undocumented Mexican immigrants have been in the country for less than five years, and many have been a part of U.S. society for over twenty years.

In spite of these statistics, indicating Mexicans' strong links to the United States and long-term contributions to its economic output, legal and societal stigma, including disparaging myths and clichés, seems to mark immigrants from Mexico as "more undocumented" than those from other countries. Mexicans comprised 52 percent of the total undocumented population but 65 percent of those deported in 2015.[3] Mexicans are also subjected to expedited repatriation, wherein those detained illegally crossing the border from Mexico or Canada can be immediately returned to their countries of origin without any judicial process.

"That's something I've called 'Mexican exclusion,'" says Carlos Spector. "There aren't waves of migrants coming from the Canadian border and being deported, right? That

provision is aimed at Mexico . . . to prevent Mexico's humanitarian crisis from being reflected in granting political
asylum." U.S. immigration court judges, Carlos says, classify the violence suffered by asylum petitioners as criminal
activity rather than political violence, despite the fact that
"the crime is being committed by the state . . . They recognize abuses in Cuba, Venezuela, all over the place, but not
Mexico."

Since its founding, the United States has presented itself to
the world as a just, fair nation that opens its arms to whoever
sets foot on its land in search of freedom and prosperity.
Nonetheless, until just before World War II, there was no
legal measure in place through which someone seeking
asylum could apply for it. After the war, when international
norms on the issue were standardized, U.S. law began to
guarantee rights to certain individuals as refugees, but generally on the basis of economic, commercial, or political criteria, rather than human or civil rights. The United States has
accepted 3 million refugees, but the vast majority of these
have come from only three countries: Cuba, Vietnam, and
the former Soviet Union. In the United States, "refugee"
almost always means "refugee from Communism."[4] The
United Nations Refugee Convention was ratified in 1951
and the United States signed the protocol defining refugees
in 1967, but for decades U.S. policy remained entrenched in
Cold War politics.

Several episodes illustrate U.S. policy toward those who
knock on the door seeking refuge. During the 1930s, for
example, President Franklin D. Roosevelt relied on the
immigrant quota system in effect at the time to justify U.S.

refusal to accept refugees from Nazi Germany. After the war, the Allies had to decide what to do about the 1 million people displaced from occupied territories. The United States created the Displaced Persons Act (DPA), agreeing to admit 205,000 refugees between 1948 and 1950. After that, approximately 80,000 Jewish refugees were also accepted through an amendment to the law, but over 70 percent of those were from the Soviet Union or Eastern Europe.[5]

Several years later, after the Cuban Revolution in 1959, the attorney general's office exercised its discretion to conditionally admit, or parole, thousands of Cubans who had abandoned the island for the United States. Through the Cuban Adjustment Act of 1966, a legal remedy was created specifically for this population, and any Cuban who had been present in the United States for one year could be granted permanent residency immediately. In addition, various federal assistance programs made it easier for the Cuban community to adjust and assimilate to life in the United States.[6]

This policy of open arms for Cubans contrasts sharply with policies in place for refugees from Haiti, a neighboring Caribbean island. During the 1970s, thousands of Haitians fled their country because of the harsh repression of dictator François Duvalier's regime. Like the Cubans, many left on small rafts or rickety boats cobbled together from whatever materials they had on hand. They made the treacherous journey and arrived in the United States seeking asylum.

As one would expect, the cases started to pile up. The U.S. government created the Haitian Program to deal with the 6,000 to 7,000 cases that had accumulated at the INS in Miami since mid-1978.[7] But the number of pending cases was rising not because the government did not have the capacity to process them, but rather because of a deliberate policy of addressing the long line of Haitian citizens at a snail's pace. Duvalier was a U.S. ally, after all. As with other countries in past decades, openly admitting that his government was creating political refugees would have contradicted U.S. diplomatic policy.

In July 1978, the INS established that Haitian refugees would be considered "economic," not political refugees. This classification dramatically reduced their likelihood of qualifying for political asylum. To discourage Haitians from trying to immigrate in the future, the INS recommended that they be detained upon their arrival in the United States, refused work permits while their cases were pending—if cases were opened for them at all—and processed and deported as soon as possible. What followed was a disaster: under the new program, refugees were interviewed at a rate of forty per day, with agents who had received no training in political asylum. Almost 40,000 applications were processed under the program, and each and every applicant was denied political asylum.

With the Refugee Act in 1980, the United States finally created a policy addressing refuge and asylum that, in accordance with United Nations policy, would treat everyone facing political persecution equally. The new policy was put to the test almost immediately with the worsening Haitian refugee crisis, as well as the arrival of thousands of Cuban refugees on the shores of southern Florida after Fidel Castro eased restrictions on migrating by sea. Between April and September 1980, approximately 125,000 Cubans left the island in a mass exodus known as the Mariel Boatlift, named for the seaside town from which many of them departed. Maintaining the approach to asylum of his predecessors, President Jimmy Carter's administration accepted Cuban migrants from the Mariel Boatlift as political refugees, while the Haitians were denied refugee status and considered to be fleeing for economic reasons.[8] During those months, the deaths of Haitians who drowned before reaching Florida's coast were largely ignored by the media.

In September 1981, president Ronald Reagan declared that Haitian immigrants represented "a serious national problem detrimental to the interests of the United States." Through an agreement with Duvalier's government, the Reagan administration allowed the U.S. Coast Guard to block boats carrying Haitian immigrants from entering U.S. waters and return them to Haiti. This was the first such agreement of its kind. By the end of 1990, 23,000 Haitians had been detained at sea under the new policy. Only eight were granted asylum. In 1991, a boat carrying Haitian refugees to the United States stopped to rescue some Cubans whose boat had sunk. When the Coast Guard intercepted them, the boat filled with Haitians was returned to Haiti with everyone on board, except the Cubans, who were taken to Florida.

In 1994 an energy crisis prompted another mass exodus from Cuba while a military coup that had brought Jean-Bertrand Aristide to power three years earlier provoked an exodus from Haiti. As thousands died at sea, a federal judge ordered U.S. president George H.W. Bush to suspend his policy of repatriating Haitians. Refugees in boats intercepted at sea were taken to the Guantanamo Naval Base in Cuba. By late 1994, 50,000 refugees were being held at the base, at a cost of between $500,000 and $1 million per day. A massive repatriation process began. Three-quarters of Haitians, even minors who were traveling alone, returned to Haiti "voluntarily." In 1995 the 20,000 Cubans who had been held at Guantanamo were brought to the United States, and the "wet foot, dry foot" policy began. (Those caught at sea were returned to Cuba, while those who made it to land qualified for expedited permanent resident status.)

This disparity in granting asylum has been a constant in U.S. immigration politics for decades. Cubans, Venezuelans, Syrians, Chinese, and Colombians who cite a fear for their lives or safety, offer a marketable skill to benefit the economy, or are attempting to reunify their families are more likely to be admitted. Meanwhile, Hondurans, Salvadorans, Guatemalans, Haitians, and Mexicans have a much lower chance of being approved for asylum and few alternative avenues for legally entering the country. Shifting economic, trade, ideological, and military alliances as well as political affiliations and rivalries among nations determine who deserves protection. When it comes to matters of asylum, geography is destiny.

The last major immigration reform legislation to be passed in the United States was signed in 1986 and established that only immigrants who had arrived in the country before January 1, 1982, and could prove it would qualify for legal status. This measure left out most Central American immigrants who had fled violence in their countries after the Sandinista victory in Nicaragua in 1979, when the rightist governments in El Salvador and Guatemala stepped up their campaigns against leftist guerrillas and their presumed sympathizers among the civilian population, including through repression of religious groups and unarmed activists. In Guatemala, hundreds of indigenous villages were destroyed in what is now openly acknowledged as an act of genocide, and millions of people were internally displaced. Between 1984 and 1990, 45,000 Salvadorans, 48,000 Nicaraguans, and 9,500 Guatemalans applied for asylum. Of the estimated 500,000 to 850,000 Salvadorans who were in the United States in 1986, only 146,000 had been in the country for at least four years.[9]

The United States opposed Nicaragua's leftist revolutionary government and supported the right-wing regimes in El Salvador and Guatemala; this meant that 26 percent of the petitions from Nicaraguans but only 2.6 percent of the Salvadorans and 1.8 percent of the Guatemalans were approved.[10] This held true for immigrants from other countries that the United States considered enemies: 73 percent of Syrians and 52 percent of Chinese, for example, were admitted.[11] In contrast, many Central American refugees were arrested at the border and returned to Mexico without even the opportunity to request asylum.

This lopsided treatment, on top of the worsening situation in Central America, sparked the growth of an important support network in the United States, including the Sanctuary Movement, which offered refuge and help to thousands fleeing violence in the 1980s. Some organizations were started by refugees themselves, such as the Central American Refugee Center (CARECEN), founded in 1983 and later renamed the Central American Resource Center. These were the first organizations to question and challenge the lack of rights for undocumented immigrants in the public sphere. Increasing emphasis was placed on the fact that U.S. intervention was one of the principal causes of the violence that prompted the exodus from Central America: "We're coming here because you were there." Activist groups called for the withdrawal of military aid to the Contras in Nicaragua and the governments of El Salvador and Guatemala. And social activist organizations filed a lawsuit, *American Baptist Churches v. Thornburgh*, which resulted in the so-called ABC settlement; as a result, through a long process that would take years for some, thousands of asylum cases were reopened in 1990, giving Salvadorans and Guatemalans another chance at legal residency. Among other things, the Immigration Act of 1990, also known as IMMACT, created Temporary Protected Status (TPS), which granted work permits to immigrants from countries affected by war or natural disasters. The permits were valid for eighteen months, and then could be renewed.

TPS for Salvadorans was extended a few times but then discontinued in 1995 after a peace treaty was signed in El Salvador, ending the civil war. At that time there were around 1 million Salvadorans living in the United States, half of whom had legal status, and 90,000 to 190,000 of whom had TPS.[12] Immigration reforms in 1996 put new obstacles in place for asylum seekers, among them giving every immigration agent the authority to deny them the opportunity to present their case to a judge, or to lock them up in detention while their cases were reviewed. When the TPS program ended, many Salvadorans once again went forward with asylum petitions that had been put on hold, but were confronted with a tremendous backlog in immigration courts. This resulted in extensive bureaucratic paperwork, followed by extremely long wait times while their applications were processed and a dark threat of deportation hung over their day-to-day lives. In 2001, the Immigration and Naturalization Service (INS) estimated that it could take as long as twenty years to process the 200,000 applications pending for Central Americans.[13]

Between 1999 and 2003, the approval rating for Salvadoran and Guatemalan asylum applicants hovered between 7 and 11 percent, a figure similar to what it had been in the 1980s, which had prompted the ABC settlement. Finally, after devastating earthquakes in El Salvador in 2001 and Haiti in 2011, a new TPS went into effect to afford some relief to undocumented immigrants from those countries, though it offered them neither permanent residency nor an eventual pathway to citizenship.[14] As Aviva Chomsky puts it in her book *Undocumented: How Immigration Became Illegal*, "Immigration law revisions have continued the pattern of creating new ways of punishing illegality, while concomitantly creating sometimes unexpected and apparently arbitrary new avenues for legalization."

# 6

## Giving Up Freedom to Save Your Life

The Eloy Detention Center is surrounded by three rows of electrified fence with barbed wire at the top. A dirt road leads to a parking lot some distance from the entrance. When I get out of the car, I walk over the lot covered in pebbles, feeling oddly vulnerable without the objects I usually carry with me. No one can enter the Detention Center with a handbag, cell phone, keys, cash, or dark sunglasses, nor a belt, any jewelry, an overcoat, or wearing a low-cut top. I cannot refer to the Detention Center as a jail, prison, correctional facility, or penal institution: the people held there have not been put on trial or sentenced, so, according to the law, they cannot be detained under prison-like conditions.

The waiting room is an irregular polygon devoid of chairs, tables, any adornment, or comfort of any sort. The space can hold up to thirty people. A man hands out numbers to each visitor. Visiting hours begin at eight o'clock in the morning. It's 8:40, and I am number fifty-two.

The number of children in the room surprises me. They are dressed up as if they're going to a party—checkered shirts and dress pants, flouncy dresses, hair carefully styled in neat braids and curls. The children try to have fun, in a space where there is no room for games. They talk to each other in English, but the adults who accompany them speak in Spanish.

A man comes over to me and asks for my help filling in the form. In the space marked "Name of detainee," he writes his brother's name. Where it says "Name of visitor," he writes his own. In the space marked "Name of Minor Visitor," he writes the same name as the detainee.

"He's my nephew, my brother's son. He's four years old. He came to visit his dad. They have the same name."

The minutes tick by, and no new numbers are called. Since we're all stuck there waiting in the same room, we begin to talk to each other to pass the time. Janet, who's number fifty-nine, just got in a few hours ago from Dallas, along with her thirteen-year-old daughter. Just the day before, they had received a phone call. Janet's mother, who had crossed the border undocumented from Tijuana, was taken into custody and transferred to Eloy. Janet does not speak English. By law she is supposed to be assigned an interpreter, but she doesn't dare ask for one. She brought her daughter with her to translate and use a computer. Because soon, she was told, she would need to find a lawyer. Juan Carlos, who left San Diego at three in the morning to get to Eloy by eight, has come to see his niece.

"We brought her so she could see her mother," he says, glancing downward. I look down and see a little girl with jet-black hair wearing a white-and-blue dress, smiling up at me. She is seven years old. "She's my niece's daughter."

He tells me his niece has been in detention for five months.

Every year the Corrections Corporation of America (CCA) receives $1.7 billion in contracts for operating prisons and detention centers. Still, in Eloy, they charge you for everything. You are not allowed to enter the visiting area with any cash, but there are vending machines. At the entrance, a visitor can purchase a card that costs five dollars. That is just for the card, there is no credit on it. In order to use it for purchases, you have to pay even more. Juan Carlos asks me to help him get one. The day before, his niece had called him and asked him to bring money so he could buy her a "burrito" from one of the vending machines.

"Can you imagine what they must be eating in here, that would make you want one of those disgusting burritos?" he asks rhetorically.

Three hours later, after passing through a metal detector, the visitors are shown into another waiting room. There, an employee shouts out the names of the detainees, and then, through two more doors (six since the entrance to the building), you get to the visiting room.

Looking around the shoebox-shaped room, I spot Yamil sitting toward the back. His khaki uniform makes him look even thinner; his hair cut short in a buzz close to his scalp brings out his shining eyes, like two black cherries. We have never met, but when I catch his eye we recognize each other. In this room, with children wrapped around their fathers' necks, a young woman holding her boyfriend close, and the three young men who take turns kissing their little cousin on the cheek, people who greet each other only with their eyes are the exception. Yamil stands up and smiles at me, and we sit down and get ready to talk. A woman in a uniform delivers a stern ultimatum: *fifty minutes*.

Yamil invites me to sit down at one of the tables. He warns me that we cannot sit on the same side of the table, we have to sit across from each other. Only minors under the age of eighteen are allowed to sit close to the detained. We have barely sat down when, in a rapid-fire move like something out of a movie, Yamil pulls out a small object and puts it on the table. The look in his eyes urges me to take it, fast. So I grab it just as quickly as he had put it down, and look down at it in my hand. It's a red-and-white ring fashioned out of pieces of cookie wrappers and empty bags of chips from the vending machines. It has been sculpted into a pattern forming connecting letters that spell my name. He explains that this is the sort of thing one learns to do in a place like Eloy.

Yamil tells me bits and pieces about his life, and at times he seems relaxed, but at some moments he seems to be trying to look strong. He has lost weight since he's been here, but he says he is in excellent physical condition. He tells me what a normal day there is like: he gets up, plays soccer—his great passion—takes a shower, plays some chess or dominoes, sometimes he helps out in the library, sometimes he helps in the kitchen. That routine only changes if you get punished. In that case, a detainee is taken to "the hole," a solitary confinement cell, with no windows, where they are only taken out in handcuffs for a half hour per day. Once, he tells me, another detainee tried to start a fight with him, and Yamil got blamed for it. He was in "the hole" for fifteen days.

"But it wasn't so bad. It's dark and it gets really cold, but you don't have to see anybody there."

I am the first visitor Yamil has had in sixteen months, since shortly after he arrived at the Immigration Detention Center in Eloy. His wife and son came to visit him a week after he was first detained here, but because they live so far away in Kansas and don't have much money, they haven't been able to come back. So there are no kids clinging to his neck, no hugs, no kisses on the cheek, no impatiently looking forward to Visiting Day on Saturday for Yamil. In spite of it all, this forty-four-year-old man originally from Durango, Mexico, is locked up here of his own free will.

What would make somebody choose to spend over a year in a shared prison cell in the United States, rather than live in freedom in Mexico?

"Hope," he answers quickly. "So I can give a better life to my family, to my son. Or just a life. Back there, something could happen at any moment."

On January 26, 2012, Yamil was kidnapped by municipal police officers in Torreón, the city where he lived. He paid a ransom, lost his business, and later survived an attack from an armed assailant. His son was beaten up. A year later, Yamil and his wife Claudia came to a decision: they had to leave their country. They left behind the little they still had. Claudia went first, and a few weeks later Yamil followed, crossing the border separating Mexico and the United States and turning himself in to immigration authorities at the gate in Nogales, where he presented an application for asylum. That was in 2013.

Five sets of locked doors and a tall fence separate Yamil from life on the outside. There are four locked doors between the visiting room and his cellblock. Even so, he says he is prepared to stay there for as long as it takes.

"You get used to everything once you're in here," he says. "You learn to see things in a different way, to be more tolerant with people, to be patient." He flashes a smile. His face changes totally when he smiles. His eyes shine even brighter; the lines that form around his eyes give him a warm, serene expression. Yamil has the peaceful look of someone who knows the wait will be worth it.

Eloy is in the middle of nowhere. Between Phoenix and Tucson, the two biggest cities in Arizona, are 116 miles of pure desert and sky. Eloy is right in the middle. Every once in a while you pass a small mountain dappled with cacti that makes it seem as if you are actually getting somewhere as you drive along the seemingly endless Interstate 10, the highway that runs from the Pacific coast in California all the way to the Atlantic in Florida. The most visible landmarks along the way are signs for McDonald's, Burger King, and Love gas stations, which appear every 6 to 12 miles.

It is the third Saturday in February, and tumbleweeds are buffeted aimlessly in the wind. That same desert wind makes the trailers on the eighteen-wheelers shimmy while their drivers listen to country music on the radio as they race down the road, or tune in to La Campesina, the station that plays *corridos* and ballads known as "regional Mexican" music here.

After taking the "Casa Grande" exit, a left turn puts me on a road that is barely paved and covered in a fine sandy dust that blankets this rugged landscape where the Akimel and Pee Posh tribes once lived. Now the Indians live on the Río Gila reservation, and the only people out on these dusty roads fall into two categories: locals who live on the isolated ranches, and people on their way to the complex of cement buildings in the heart of the desert. The buildings are three correctional facilities and an immigration detention center known as Eloy. In the middle of nowhere, these four buildings contain 5,000 lives, walled in by barbed wire and electrified fences.

Eloy is one of the six detention centers in Arizona operated by the Corrections Corporation of America (CCA), the private company that manages most of the prisons under subcontract in the United States.[1] Eloy has 1,596 beds, and is filled with men and women accused of being on this side of the border without a piece of paper. For the past thirty years, the CCA—which changed its name to CoreCivic in October 2016—has made millions in profits by holding immigrants in detention while they wait for their cases to be decided by a judge. Yamil is one of these immigrants.

When Yamil first got to Eloy, he knew what he was in for: six weeks earlier, his wife, Claudia, had been in the same place. I hear two versions of the story: one from Claudia in Kansas, where she returned after a judge released her while her asylum case was being decided, and Yamil's version in the visiting room in Eloy. Each one shares details of their lives together, precious memories they cherish during these long months of separation.

Claudia's family moved to Durango from Tijuana when she was ten years old. They lived there for three years until her father was murdered, forcing the family to flee Mexico. Claudia, her three sisters, and her mother started their lives over in Wichita, Kansas. By a coincidence that some people might call destiny, Yamil, also from Durango, moved there too when he was nineteen after deciding to migrate north.

Yamil and Claudia met at a dance in Wichita in September 1998. They got married four months later, and their son was born in 2000. Claudia started baking and selling cakes and volunteering at their son's school, while Yamil worked as a painter and played soccer in a semi-professional league.

The life they built together came crashing down in 2005. One day, as he was driving home, Yamil was pulled over for a minor traffic violation. When the police officer asked to see his identification, the authorities discovered that the document Yamil presented was false. Even though his son is a U.S. citizen, neither he nor Claudia had been able to legalize their status, and Yamil was deported. Then Claudia had to make a hard choice: stay in Wichita, in her home with her son, or go to Mexico so the three of them could be together. In 2006, she and Yamil Jr. went to join her husband in Torreón, Mexico, where his family was then living.

The culture shock they had both experienced as arrivals to the United States took hold once again. Claudia and her husband tried to adapt to a way of life that was no longer theirs, while their son found himself in a completely unknown world. The boy started having problems in school, and was bullied for being an American. Claudia and Yamil could not find work, and the violence that roiled the country during Felipe Calderón's six-year presidential term started flaring up in the area. Gun battles and killings became a part of everyday life: one day Claudia and Yamil Jr. saw two bodies hanging from a bridge. Then extortion became commonplace. And one day, it was their turn.

"I will never forget it, it was January 26, 2012, my son's birthday," Claudia recalls angrily. She tells me the whole story over the phone. "We were in a very difficult financial situation. I was teaching classes at night at the university and Yamil ran a little hamburger place." The family had recently purchased a used truck. That day two men approached the couple and insisted the truck had been reported stolen, and that they needed to confiscate it and take Yamil with them. A few hours later the family got a phone call demanding ransom for Yamil's release. A cousin lent them the money, and he was set free. But a few weeks later, two other men pulled him over while he was driving and demanded money before they would let him go; then one day, armed gunmen took the truck.

"After that, for three days, they would come by and check out my business," Yamil tells me, his arms resting on the table in the visiting room at Eloy. We have been talking for a half hour, and this is the only point in the conversation where a shadow passes over his face. He doesn't seem bitter, but this is clearly something he can't forget. "I had to shut it down."

A few months later, the couple went to the municipal offices to file a complaint: in an extreme act of bullying, their son had been beaten up by six other boys, who called him "gringo" and "pocho." As Yamil gave his testimony, he recognized one of the police officers. It was one of the men who had stolen his truck.

In July 2013, Claudia and her son joined a group of young adults who had also grown up in the United States, returned to Mexico for one reason or another, and now wanted to go back to the country they considered theirs. They passed through the turnstile at the border crossing into the United States, and requested political asylum. A few weeks later, Yamil made the same trip with another group. Given that it is up to a judge's discretion whether to release the asylum petitioner on their own recognizance or hold them in detention, that decision varies case by case. Claudia and their son were released, but Yamil was not. And even though he could voluntarily return to Mexico at any time, he chooses to stay in prison.

Yamil worries about his case. Other detainees have been released on their own recognizance, but the lawyer handling his case is not optimistic, he tells me. Still, he tries not to despair. March 30 will be the first in a series of appearances before a judge. Claudia and his son will come to accompany him, he tells me with the same unguarded emotion he reveals whenever he talks about his family: the time when he and Claudia were dating and got caught in the rain; the time when the family traveled throughout the United States for Yamil's soccer games. It's only when he tells me about his last Christmas that a lump rises in his throat, and he can't continue. Two seemingly endless minutes tick by.

"When I talk with them, I know we're doing the right thing," he says. "My son says he misses me, and I tell him to stay strong. Now he's playing soccer at school. They're going to have a tournament, and he's the captain of the team." He glows with pride. "And I feel fine about Claudia. I sent her a picture of myself a little while ago, so she could see that I'm okay, I'm in good shape. So she'll see I'm worth the wait," he says with a playful laugh.

When evening comes in this part of the Arizona desert, twilight paints the sky in brilliant oranges, magentas, and violets, warming the clouds. The light kisses the golden, arid land, in a gorgeous, wide-open panorama of light and freedom. But from the concrete buildings in Eloy, the detainees can only catch a glimpse of this spectacular sunset through the narrow windows facing west. In Eloy, the boundless freedom of the American Dream barely filters through the bars.

For detainees in an immigration detention center, having a lawyer is critical. One of the system's problems is the separation between the immigration courts and the criminal justice system. Immigration courts are administrative courts, so the legal and ethical system designed to guarantee a fair process to those accused of committing a crime does not apply— unless the individual with a case in immigration court is also facing criminal charges. People have fewer rights in the immigration detention system, and fewer resources to ensure that they can exercise the rights they do have. Immigrants have the right to be represented by an attorney, but they have no right to a lawyer at no cost, financed by the state. Many in immigration detention therefore do not know that they have a right to legal representation, or do not know how to get a lawyer, or cannot afford one. As a result, 84 percent of people in deportation proceedings have no attorney, and only 3 percent of those without representation win the right to stay in the country.[2]

These myriad deficiencies facilitate abuse and prompt some immigrants to leave the country voluntarily rather than risking a deportation on their record, assuming that having a "clean" immigration record will allow them to enter the country legally in the future. (A person cannot reenter the United States for ten years after being deported.) Many detainees are unaware of legal mechanisms that would allow them to stay in the country. Some opt for voluntary removal just to escape a prolonged detention. And unlike people arrested under criminal charges, immigrants are rarely eligible to be released on bail.

Deportation proceedings for those who reject voluntary removal are often lengthy, and while they wait for a final decision, immigrants remain locked in detention centers. An Amnesty International study found that although the average wait time was ten months, some people had waited as long as four years for a judge to issue a ruling.

In January 2012, Maria Odom, then executive director of the Catholic Legal Immigration Network, was explaining in an interview why she had been working pro bono for years as an immigration attorney, providing representation for those unable to pay.

"Through pro bono work, you get to know the most incredible people you could ever meet," she said. "And you'll learn things you wouldn't learn in your regular law practice. You grow, and you'll work on the cases that will define you as a lawyer for the rest of your professional career."

With a tawny complexion, short dark-brown hair, warm eyes and an open smile, Maria talked enthusiastically about her day-to-day work at one of the most respected organizations protecting asylum seekers and refugees in the United States. At that moment Odom, originally from Puerto Rico, probably had no idea that eight months later, her career path would lead to the federal government. But that September, she was appointed Citizenship and Immigration Services Ombudsman for the U.S. Department of Homeland Security (DHS), responsible for improving the quality of service and advocating for the rights of those processed by that department, including refugees and asylum seekers.

In her annual report presented in June 2015,[3] Odom admitted that there was a substantial backlog in affirmative asylum cases pending before the U.S. Customs and Immigration Service (USCIS), which "has led to lengthy case processing times for tens of thousands of asylum seekers." According to the report, the increase in applications based on credible, reasonable fears had compelled the department to redirect resources that had been previously earmarked for affirmative asylum cases; that, on top of the rising number of new cases, had caused the backlog. There were 9,274 affirmative asylum cases pending by the end of 2011. By the end of 2014, that number had ballooned to 73,103, an increase of 700 percent. In 2011, there were 11,337 cases based on credible, reasonable fear. By 2014, that number had quintupled, reaching 51,001. USCIS, the report explained, had taken measures to address the situation such as hiring additional personnel and adjusting scheduling priorities. But, Odom wrote, "the backlog continues to mount."

According to USCIS procedure, asylum officials rule on the declarations of credible and reasonable fear to determine if asylum applicants meet the requirements for having their case decided by an immigration judge. Since many of these applicants are in detention, the USCIS gives these cases priority. Up until December 26, 2014, the agency prioritized the most recent applications over the ones that had been waiting a long time, partly to discourage what they considered to be a "frivolous use" of this legal measure to get a work permit quickly.

Between October 1, 2014, and March 5, 2015, of the approximately 600 requests for assistance[4] related to refuge and asylum received by the office of the ombudsman, 68 percent involved applicants who had yet to be scheduled for their first interview in the asylum process. Twenty-five percent had completed their interviews but still had not received a final decision on their cases. Many applicants also expressed fear for the safety and well-being of family members outside the United States, whose only possibility of entering the United States depended on a successful outcome of their asylum petitions.

Of the applicants who requested the ombudsman's intervention in their cases, 26 percent had been waiting for two years for their cases to be resolved, 27 percent between eighteen months and two years, 29 percent between one year and eighteen months, and 16 percent between six months and a year. In only one of the cases requesting intervention had the applicant been waiting less than six months after initially applying for asylum.

After receiving these complaints, Odom's office contacted the authorities in charge of asylum at different points in the application process to evaluate possible measures to address pending interviews and to minimize the damaging effects of prolonged wait times. One recommendation that resulted was to hire more staff. USCIS went from 203 officers in 2013 to 350 in 2015, although there is a high turnover rate; the average asylum officer stays in the position for only fourteen months. New scheduling priorities were also established for interviews: rescheduled interviews were now first priority; applications from children were second priority; and all the other cases pending would be processed in the order they were received. Critics of these changes worried that they would attract false applications and that adjustments to the credible fear interview process could compromise the effectiveness and overall quality of the interviews.

I asked Claudia if she had ever heard about the ombudsman for the immigrant detention center system, charged with ensuring that their rights were protected. Claudia had never heard the word "ombudsman."

# 7

# The Business of Locking Up Migrants

"Hello. This is Delmy, at the Detention Center."

Delmy Calderón's voice reaches me from Texas, where it must already feel like Christmas, just like it does here in California. I have been waiting for Delmy's call all morning. But I had not expected the voice on the other end to sound so weak. Maybe it was because Delmy and nine other women detained with her were three days into a hunger strike. Or maybe it was because, after six months in detention, hopelessness was gaining ground.

"I'm desperate. Sometimes I feel like I can't take it anymore," she tells me, her voice breaking, and I'm afraid she might hang up. The people detained at the center cannot accept telephone calls, so I had to leave her a message and deposit money in a Western Union account linked to the phone at the center so that Delmy could call me back. "I won't leave here because it's not safe to go back to my country, but I don't know how much longer I can stand this."

Delmy, forty-two, is one of 800 migrants held at the immigration detention center in El Paso, officially known as a "processing center": a complex of buildings located between a golf course and the airport. There, people without documents who have been arrested by immigration agents, or who have voluntarily surrendered in U.S. territory or at a border entry point and have applied for a humanitarian visa or political asylum, wait for a judge to decide their case and either let them go free or deport them back to their countries of origin. Most of them are from Mexico, but there are plenty of detainees from Central American countries, and even some from China, India, and Australia.

Delmy is from El Salvador, where she lived with her four children and owned a restaurant. Although they were hardly wealthy, her family had been financially stable. Going to the United States had never even crossed her mind until July 2013, when members of the MS 18 gang demanded money for letting her run her business. Delmy told them she could not pay them the amount they asked for. The gang threatened to hurt her family. Just a week before, a neighbor had been murdered by the same gang.

Delmy decided to close her restaurant and head north. After crossing the border into the United States, she was arrested by border patrol agents. Delmy explained her situation, requested asylum, and just a few days later was interviewed by a judge to establish that she had a "credible fear"—a real reason to fear for her life. The judge decided in her favor and assigned her a case number. Following asylum protocol, a legal process then began which could take as long as seven years, given the current backlog: in late 2016 there were over half a million asylum cases pending, and a total of 277 immigration judges in the entire country.

While they wait for their cases to make their way to court, asylum applicants stay in the United States. If they do not have a criminal record and do not pose a threat to public safety, they are released under their own recognizance and given a temporary work permit. These applicants are called "low priority." At the end of the process, if they are granted asylum, they are granted residency. If asylum is denied, they are returned to their home country.

After passing her "credible fear" interview, Delmy was taken to the detention center in El Paso in September. Because of her low priority status, a judge should have granted her release within a matter of days. But the weeks passed, and she remained there. A week before Christmas, she decided to go on a hunger strike.

Cases like Delmy's are not unusual. A few days before I spoke with her on the phone, members of Dreamactivist, a national organization of undocumented youth who perform acts of civil disobedience to call for the passage of a law to legalize their status, went undercover in the El Paso detention center. Santiago García, a member of the group, turned himself in to immigration agents on November 21 to report from the inside on what it's like for people who spend weeks and months behind bars while waiting for a resolution to their case.

In a phone conversation from inside the detention center, Santiago, then twenty-three, told me about some of the things he had seen. There were at least a hundred other cases like Delmy's—people who had passed the credible fear test before a judge, but were still being held behind bars.

"I've met people in here who should have been released months ago. They've been in here as long as nine months, locked up, and a lot of them don't even know that legally they could have been let out by now," Santiago told me. "These people didn't come here to find the American dream, they came because they had to leave everything to save themselves from violence, or because of their sexual orientation. If they get deported, death is waiting for them in their country."

Dreamactivist had tried to call attention to the cases they found at the El Paso detention center in September, in an action called #Dream30. Thirty undocumented young people who had grown up in the United States and been deported back to Mexico took part in the action. They turned themselves in to immigration agents at the border crossing in Laredo, Texas, requested asylum, and were then transported to the detention center in El Paso. But something very unusual happened: all of the thirty Dreamactivist cases were resolved in less than six weeks.

Dreamactivist says their members were treated differently from the rest because of political, economic, and even media-related factors. "We think in our case, because they know we were trying to organize people inside and explain their rights to them, and because they were getting calls from the media about our cases, they released us as soon as possible," said Santiago, who was released less than two weeks after being detained, under the same low priority category as Delmy.

Brenda Castro, then twenty-three, had a very different experience. In October 2013, Brenda had to leave her life in Juárez. Her brother Santos, twenty-one, had witnessed a murder at a business near his home, and he had been wounded by a gunshot in the incident. He was taken to the hospital for treatment, where he had to give a statement on what he had seen. A short time later, the family got a message: they were all going to be killed. They did not think twice. Brenda, her parents, Santos, his wife, and their newborn baby girl went to the border gate to request asylum. Brenda's mother, sister-in-law, and her baby were released on their own recognizance. But Brenda, Santos, and their father were still behind bars a month and a half later, even though they had passed the "credible fear" test at the beginning of November.

"I went on a hunger strike to see if they would let me out quick that way," Brenda tells me over the phone, after Delmy spreads the word to her fellow detainees that a journalist is interested in their stories. "They say if you stop eating and start getting sick, they rush to let you out, because they don't want anyone to die in here."

The third woman I spoke with, Rosario Hernández, forty-six, was also born in Juárez, and had a story similar to Brenda's. One day several armed men paid a visit to her son-in-law, and told him they were going to kill his entire family. The Hernández family went to the Judicial Police, but were told that all they could do was register a complaint.

"I told them, if we did that, they would come back and kill us all over again," Rosario says firmly, sounding a bit more composed than her companions in detention with whom I spoke. "So the police officers themselves told us we should go surrender to U.S. authorities. We came here, we passed the credible fear interview on September 15, and look, three months later we're still in here."

After talking to the women on hunger strike, I called Leticia Zamarripa, spokesperson for the detention center, which is under the jurisdiction of Immigration and Customs

Enforcement (ICE). Friendly and approachable, Zamarripa acknowledges the criticisms from Dreamactivist and other activist organizations. But, she says, the lengths of time detainees spend in detention is determined not by local authorities, but by the U.S. Customs and Immigration Service (USCIS), an agency which includes the judges who are assigned to the immigrants' cases. The staff managing the detention centers deal with the consequences of the backlog caused by the federal immigration courts.

According to USCIS policy, cases are assigned to judges according to their workload, so there is no specific timeframe in place for processing cases. But most immigration lawyers agree that three weeks in detention tends to be the norm for detainees released on their own recognizance in jurisdictions like Arizona and other parts of Texas.

"Aside from the backlog in immigration courts, there's another issue," Santiago tells me a few months later. "The ones operating the detention centers are making money off of the people in there. They receive federal funds for each person, and the longer they are in there, the more money they get."

The U.S. government spends over $2 billion every year detaining undocumented immigrants. This figure doubled from 2004 to 2013. For each day that a person is held in detention, the operator of the prison receives $164, and up to $298 for family detention centers. The El Paso center receives more than $130,000 a day to keep its 800 detainees confined within four walls.

The immigration detention system in the United States has grown drastically, from fewer than 10,000 beds in 1999 to

34,000 in 2014 in 250 centers, according to the American Civil Liberties Union (ACLU). In 2010 the Department of Homeland Security (DHS) held 363,000 immigrants in detention throughout the country. Six of every ten of these detainees were held in prisons operated by two thirty-year-old private companies: Correction Corporation of America (CCA), now CoreCivic, and GEO Group.

Headquartered in Nashville, Tennessee, CoreCivic has over 15,000 employees. In 2013 the company reported income of over $700 million and a profit of $300 million, of which 100 percent came from government contracts funded by taxpayers. According to a shareholder report, the president and CEO of CoreCivic, Damon T. Hininger, who is paid an annual salary of over $700,000, made over $3.2 million in 2013, including earnings from company stock and three other types of compensation. For their part, GEO Group, with headquarters in Boca Raton, Florida, is the leader in the international market, with almost one hundred detention centers and 18,000 employees in the United States and around the world, according to their corporate reports. Operating under the name Wackenhut Corrections Corporation in its early years, GEO reported earnings of $1.5 billion in 2013. Together, the two corporations have annual earnings of over $3 billion, of which at least $2 billion come from taxpayers.

This is possible because of a policy first implemented in the 2007 Department of Homeland Security (DHS) Appropriations Act, known as the detention center quota. The provision requires ICE to hold a minimum number of detainees every year to guarantee that the private corporations that run the detention centers make a sufficient return on their investment. The measure would not have been implemented without years of intense lobbying efforts by the private prison corporations themselves. According to the Detention Watch Network (DWN), in 2013 GEO Group's lobbyists spent $1.2 million to convince Congress to act in their interest. The company spent an additional $880,000 on outside lobby groups.

In the Public Interest (ITPI), a research and policy center in Washington, D.C., focused on concessions and privatization, has analyzed private prison contracts. The center found that 65 percent of private detention center contracts include a clause requiring the contractor be paid between 80 and 100 percent of the cost of operating at full capacity, even if there are empty cells. This contractual mechanism is called a "low-crime tax," through which taxpayers guarantee that the corporations' earnings do not decrease. The states of Arizona, Louisiana, Oklahoma, and Virginia guarantee the highest prison occupation rates: between 95 and 100 percent.

A report by DWN asserts that the quotas encourage immigration agents to focus on certain populations in order to ensure that beds in the detention centers are occupied and that "Congress and ICE . . . treat immigrants as numbers to fill a quota and as products to be bought and sold." As information on the quotas has circulated more widely, other organizations have joined the call for a stop to the business of locking up immigrants. In 2014 the National Immigrant Justice Center, a human rights organization, released a series of recommendations which included eliminating quotas and substituting detention with alternatives like remote monitoring systems, which would allow people to be with their families as they wait for their cases to be resolved. Alternatives to detention such as electronic monitoring bracelets, however, would only allow prisons to charge between seventy cents and $17 per day, per person—much less than the $160 per individual held in a detention center.

The GEO Group and CoreCivic both have long histories of abuse charges, human rights violations, labor exploitation, and a lack of transparency, some of which have resulted in fines and facility closures. The most widely known episode involving CoreCivic took place at the T. Don Hutto Residential Center in Taylor, Texas, outside of Austin. The center functioned as a "family residence," holding families with children in detention until 2009, when the Obama administration closed it under pressure from activists who documented the conditions there, including children dressed in prison uniforms with no access to education or medical attention.

As for GEO, its Coke County Juvenile Justice Center, also in Texas, was sued by twelve families for "multiple rapes of minors by adults." A few of the employees were sanctioned, and the families were awarded a financial settlement, but no senior managers were punished. One of the victims, who had been raped when she was fifteen years old, committed suicide on the day the settlement was announced. In 2007 the center was closed due to unsanitary and unsafe conditions, including excessive use of pepper spray to "control" detainees, a lack of educational programs, feces in cells, unhealthy food infested with insects, and a lack of sufficient personnel to adequately manage the facility.

According to DWN, 165 people died in immigration detention centers between 2003 and 2016, mainly from heart and respiratory conditions although some from kidney failure, cancer, and suffocation. Organizations that monitor private prisons have denounced the lack of preventative care and medical treatment inside these facilities. During the same period, CoreCivic and GEO spent over $32 million combined to lobby Congress, according to Grassroots Leadership. These lobbying efforts had an effect on the Obama administration, which approved an expansion project for family detention centers and even opened two new centers in Karnes and Dilley, Texas. The first was awarded to GEO, and the second to CoreCivic.

What do people held in immigration detention centers do all day? Their daily routine takes them from the dormitory to the cafeteria, and back again. Meals are served at 6:30 a.m., 11:30 a.m., and 4:30 p.m., and after meals they go back to their beds. The alternative to this monotony is the detainee voluntary work program.

According to ICE policy, this program was designed to give detainees "the opportunity to earn money" and so that "the negative impact of confinement will be reduced because of improved morale, and fewer incidents requiring corrective action." Detainees can opt to work in the kitchen or clean the dormitories or bathrooms. They are paid $1 per day for their work—a real bargain, considering the minimum wage is $7.25 per hour. The great irony here is that some detainees who are there and wind up "working" for the federal government were initially detained because they were found to be working illegally without documentation. To organizations monitoring the corporations that run the immigrant detention centers, the creation of the work program has little to do with addressing human rights concerns, but rather resembles a cost-cutting measure intended to boost profits.

On October 22, 2014, a group of people detained at the Immigration Detention Center in Aurora, Colorado, operated by GEO, filed a class action lawsuit against the corporation, claiming that they had been exploited as cheap or free labor while they were detained. The plaintiffs, Alejandro Menocal, Marcos Brambila, Grisel Xahuentitla, Hugo Hernández, Lourdes Argueta, Jesús Gaytán, Olga Alexaklina, Dagoberto Vizguerra, and Demetrio Valerga, all detainees or former detainees who were imprisoned and employed by the GEO Group, filed the suit on behalf of themselves and others in similar situations for unpaid wages and forced labor, as well as illicit enrichment.

Since according to Immigration and Customs Enforcement (ICE) directives, the work performed by those who decide to participate in the program is strictly voluntary, there has not been any legal measure put in place to stop it. That is what the lawsuit seeks to do by charging that the program results in exploitation and forced work.

The lawsuit states that "in the course of their employment by GEO, Plaintiffs and others . . . cleaned and maintained GEO's on-site medical facility, cleaned the medical facility's toilets, floors and windows, cleaned patient rooms and medical staff offices, swept, mopped, stripped, and waxed the floors of the medical facility, did medical facility laundry, swept, mopped, stripped, and waxed floors throughout the facility, did detainee laundry, prepared and served detainee meals, assisted in preparing catered meals for law enforcement events sponsored by GEO, performed clerical work for GEO, prepared clothing for newly arriving detainees, provided barber services to detainees, ran the facility's law library, cleaned the facility's intake area and solitary confinement unit, deep cleaned and prepared vacant portions of the facility for newly arriving detainees, cleaned the facility's warehouse, and maintained the exterior and landscaping of the GEO building, inter alia." They received $1 per day for their work, and those who refused to work were put in solitary confinement. They were required to clean their own cells, or "living pods," for no pay. Given the federal minimum wage, the corporations running the centers saved $28 per detainee in labor costs for every four hours of a detainee's work. GEO has responded through its spokesperson that its facilities comply with federal government rules and standards.

On February 27, 2017, at the onset of Trump's presidential term, the federal judge in charge of this case ruled that a class action lawsuit against GEO could proceed. The suit could include as many as 60,000 plaintiffs, all immigrants who have been detained in that company's facilities over the last decade.

# Part Three
# Impunity

# 8

## Preserving Memory

In one room of a one-story building, on a wide, dusty avenue of Juárez, workshops for children are held. The workshops began in 2011. Once a week, little boys and girls, four to eight years old, come through the doors of the building to attend a workshop.

They are workshops in pain.

The sessions are designed to help these children whose fathers, or mothers, or both, have been shot to death, kidnapped, stuffed into trunks, dismembered, or dumped on a deserted field to rot, or all of the above. Some of these children watched their parents being murdered. Some of them are traumatized simply because they live in Juárez.

There are also mothers in Juárez who come to the building, who have not been murdered, but easily could have been. Women who know what a bone breaking sounds like. Who get here by a miracle, and when they go home, they walk fast, looking over their shoulders. They meet up with other women in the building, as they have for the past fourteen years when Casa Amiga was founded, to offer protection and counseling to victims of domestic or gender violence. Twelve years ago, the "Juárez murders" started appearing in newspaper headlines. But now, the nature of the violence here has changed: the so-called war on narcotrafficking means that extreme violence against women has blended in with other homicides, extortions, and mass executions. Now it's not just women coming here. Men come too. And families. And children who have no families left.

Every day at Casa Amiga, proof walks through the door that no one is safe here, that the city of Juárez has been abandoned, left for dead.

It's a Monday in January 2013, late afternoon. The dusty avenue is bathed in a strange light under a grayish-pink sky, eerily underscoring the feeling of abandonment palpable throughout the city. We arrive at Casa Amiga, a building constructed of cement blocks, its outside walls painted in vibrant shades of blue, yellow, and purple. It looks entirely out of place on the avenue.

Our little group must look very odd to the locals. The two men responsible for us being here are a Mexican, a Chicano-looking professor in his fifties with expressive eyes behind glasses, and another professor, a gringo in his sixties with a slender build and a serious, formal demeanor. The three of us came from Los Angeles. A local photographer is with us, tall, with a dark complexion and a look of having seen it all—and, in fact, he has seen it all—and an American woman, an academic-activist of short stature and a bossy attitude that reminds me of the mother, played by Frances McDormand, in the film *Almost Famous*. We are just finishing up our first day of this trip—my first visit to El Paso–Juárez to do research for this book—but I feel like I have been listening to heartbreaking tales of pain for weeks. The photographer parks the car; without saying a word we get out, take a deep breath, and walk through the front door.

A few minutes later a door opens and out steps a slender woman looking much younger than her thirty-six years, her outward appearance not even hinting at her profound inner strength. With horrific stories constantly coming and going at Casa Amiga, only the strongest of the strong last long.

Irma Casas is the director of Casa Amiga. She gives us a tour, showing us the rooms filled with children's books and toys. She tells us that Casa Amiga has been serving approximately 20,000 people per year, victims of every kind of violence.

"Juárez is in a postwar situation," Irma explains, her long, chestnut hair worn loose, her fair complexion free of makeup, eyes very open, her face serious. "We are confronting the pain of children with two dead parents. We understand that the cost of what we are experiencing today will be seen in ten, twenty years." Rates of violence among minors are alarming; there are reports of attempted homicide involving eight-year-old children. In Guadalupe Valley, an area on the outskirts of Juárez where organized crime has taken over, suicide rates among young people have risen. Teens use words that didn't exist ten years ago, made up to describe new crimes: *bicicleteros* (bike thieves), *boteros*, *carjacking*. When the military began arriving in 2008, the number of human rights violations rose to the highest ever recorded; when federal forces began arriving that year, cases of sexual violence against women, including young women being raped and tortured, increased markedly.

Kent Kirkton could be the star of a TV series, and not just because of his alliterative name that sounds like it was dreamed up by a Hollywood agent. When he walks through the halls of California State University Northridge (CSUN) in Los Angeles, everyone knows him as the professor who, after spending years in the journalism department, now runs the Institute for Arts and Media. But before he was an academic, Kent—with his fair complexion, his head sparsely covered with white hair on the back and sides, with a goatee to match, his affable nature apparent in his eyes behind glasses—played other roles.

Kent was born in 1945 in Gredley, Illinois, a small Midwestern town with less than a thousand residents. At that time, half of the townspeople lived on farms, and when Kent graduated from high school in 1963, there were only thirty-six students in his graduating class. Even though they lived in a conservative community, the Kirktons could be described as progressive. Kent's father was the manager of a carpentry business, and his mother, who had started out working in a butcher shop, went on to be an assistant paralegal in a law firm. Their family hosted exchange students, and, according to Kent, his parents were closet Democrats.

After spending a few years in the military as a medical assistant and a few months on the front lines in Vietnam, Kent decided he wanted to be a photographer. He earned a master's degree at Illinois University and a doctorate in mass communications at the University of Iowa. He worked for a while at various newspapers, and then, in the eighties, he moved to California to be a professor in photojournalism at CSUN. He soon realized that Southern California had no photojournalism archives. Local newspapers like the *Los Angeles Times* had photojournalists on staff who captured thousands of images of the civil rights and Chicano movements, but only a few of those pictures were published in the paper, and the rest were thrown away.

In 1990, after jumping through many bureaucratic hoops, Kent finally got his project off the ground: the Center for Photojournalism and Visual History, which he now directs. One of his central objectives was to find images from photographers working in media made for people of color, since it was clear that coverage in the so-called "mainstream media" only focused on issues relating to the white Anglo population. With that perspective, his first collections included thousands of images by Guy Crowder, photographer for the African American daily *LA Sentinel*, and Emmon Clarke, who documented the movement to unionize farmworkers led by the Chicano activist Cesar Chavez in California. Today the institute has over 850,000 negatives and the largest collection in existence of African American photographs, as well as works donated by the fine art photographer Richard Cross documenting the wars in El Salvador and Honduras.

Kent was working on building the center's collection in 2002 when he was promoted to director of the Department of Journalism at CSUN; one of his first initiatives in that post was to start a journalism program in Spanish. He began searching for a coordinator for the project, and that's when José Luis Benavides came on the scene.

José Luis is a charming man. With dark hair and a dark complexion and soulful eyes with bags under them, he tends to wield his winsome smile as a tool of persuasion. He speaks Spanish with a light accent which could be Chicano but isn't quite; it's the classic "not from here nor there/ni de aquí ni de allá" that comes from both sides of the border.

José Luis came to CSUN by way of Texas, where he earned his master's and doctorate degrees. Originally from Mexico City, he was critical of the vacuous nature of the U.S. university system, the lack of cultural diversity in academic life, and the ignorance often found among journalists. After accepting the position of director of the Spanish journalism program from Kent, he developed a solid curriculum mainly for immigrants and the children of immigrants from Latin American countries. He hoped to work with audiences from those countries, in Spanish- or English-language media, and to focus on issues affecting the Spanish-speaking community in the United States. In 2007, José Luis founded the Spanish-language student newspaper *El Nuevo Sol*, a multimedia publication covering issues of particular interest to the Latino community, including immigration and border issues.

José Luis and Kent's meeting could not have been more fortuitous. In spite of very different backgrounds and a fifteen-year age difference, the two clicked right away. Their ideologies and visions for the future aligned perfectly, and immediately they set to work on several projects together. When Kent stepped down from his post at the Department of Journalism, José Luis took his place.

Writer and journalist Charles Bowden, who would pass away in August 2014, after our trip to Casa Amiga, spent more than a decade writing about issues and events surrounding the border. At the time of our visit, he had recently turned his attention to the violence in Juárez from the alleged war on narcotrafficking initiated by the government. Of particular interest was the economic and political relationship between the two countries: the corruption, impunity, and indifference on both sides of the border. His book *Murder City: Ciudad Juárez and the Global Economy's New Killing Fields* (Nation Books, 2011) was published to great acclaim. José Luis discovered Charles's work and mentioned it to several colleagues, including Kent. The two made arrangements for Charles to come to CSUN in November 2011 and give a talk to the journalism students.

Charles traveled to Los Angeles with his partner, Molly Molloy—the American academic-activist who would later come with us to Juárez—from their home in Las Cruces, New Mexico, a town forty minutes away from the El Paso–Juárez border. José Luis and Kent visited him there months later, coming face-to-face with the stark realities of life for those exiled by violence. They spent five days around the border and, after returning to Los Angeles, could talk about nothing but Juárez.

"We realized there is an enormous need to preserve the memory," José Luis explains to Irma and the rest of the group sitting around a table at Casa Amiga. "When violence forces people to abandon their homes to save their lives, they [the criminals] go and ransack the house and burn it down. There's nothing left, and we run the risk of people saying it never even happened in the future." After their trip to the border, he and Kent decided to create an oral history archive, collecting interviews with victims of violence in Juárez and those attempting to help them.

This is the third trip José Luis and Kent have made with the aim of preserving memory. They conduct interviews with people exiled by violence, many of whom are represented by Carlos Spector. Some of the interviews go on for hours. When they get back to Los Angeles they transcribe the recordings, translate them so that the archive is in Spanish and English, and file them with no editing. The archive includes 17,000 images as well. The plan is to keep adding as many interviews as they can get. The project has no budget; twice a year, the two professors dip into their own savings and devote their free time to traveling half the length of the border, collecting fragments of the present, in the hope that they will someday be a tool for those who want to know what happened here.

Irma, who is surprised and moved by what she hears, offers to help in any way she can, including granting access to some of Casa Amiga's files that would not violate anyone's privacy. As we have coffee and cookies, it occurs to me that we have spent the past three hours talking about murders, mutilations, and raped women. Horrific images run through my mind, and I feel physically ill. The people who have told us about these cases are outraged but not surprised. I think they don't react like the rest of us anymore. They are different, because they happen to live in Juárez.

"We are in El Paso, today is January twenty-first, and we are with Gloria Lopez."

José Luis makes sure the microphone is working and begins his interview with Gloria, who is sitting up very straight with the clip-on mic attached to her blazer lapel, facing her interviewer. Gloria is married to Saúl Reyes, the only surviving male of the ten Reyes siblings. She and their three children came with Saúl when he decided to apply for political asylum.

Gloria dressed up for the interview. She is wearing a purple blouse under a fuchsia blazer, glasses, stud earrings, and a silver necklace, her hair pulled back. She starts off talking about how she was born in Chihuahua in 1974. When she was seven years old, the family moved to Guadalupe. As with all the others who have been interviewed during this trip, Gloria's childhood includes idyllic memories of Valle de Guadalupe: it was prosperous, with plenty of jobs, people were happy to work in agriculture, and she fondly remembers her father taking her out to play in the plaza. That all ended, she recalls, when the factories started coming.

While Gloria talks and José Luis performs his role as interviewer/memory collector, Kent attends to other tasks: he takes photos of Gloria, and of José Luis, and of the two of them; he sets up a camera to record some video; he makes sure there are enough batteries. Kent does not speak any Spanish, but he understands a bit thanks to Juana, his wife of fifteen years, whose family lives in Tijuana. Gloria speaks softly; she is shy and at first her answers are brief, without elaboration. But as the interview goes on, she begins to talk more freely, emphasizing the most important parts of her story.

The story that José Luis captured that day is about how Gloria, the daughter of a family of PAN (National Action Party) supporters, fell in love with Saúl, of the Reyes brothers, the leftist PRD (Revolutionary Democratic Party) family who had a successful bakery, where the whole family worked. While they baked bread and distributed it to other businesses, the Reyes family exchanged progressive books, making sure not to discuss a book until everyone had read it. Gloria says the Reyes family's class and social consciousness fed on bread and books.

Gloria and Saúl had their first date on January 1, 1994, while in the Selva Lacandona, a group of indigenous people took up arms under the banner of the Zapatista Liberation Army. They got married a year and a half later, and lived with his parents while Saúl saved up money to build their own house. Life with Saúl and his family made Gloria understand why the activist Reyes were so vocal: if the authorities would not listen to them and the government would not satisfy the demands of their constituents, they had to speak up. Other PAN supporters accused Gloria of being a spy; she soon switched her party allegiance to PRD. The people in town knew they could count on the Reyeses. When women had a problem, they sought out Josefina, Saúl's sister, who participated in the movement demanding justice for the women who had been killed in the area.

After living with Saúl's parents for a while, Gloria and Saúl had saved up enough money to build their own house. With a pride that lights up her face in a wide smile, her glasses rising a bit higher over her cheeks, Gloria recalls how they built the house with their own hands, mixing the cement, pouring it into molds, constructing the walls, and putting in the windows. In 2000 they opened their own bakery and moved into their new house with their two-year-old son, Saúl Ernesto (his middle name an homage to Che Guevara) and Saúl's growing book collection. Two more sons followed. Then the Reyes assassinations began in 2008. Magdalena, Elías, and Luisa were kidnapped and killed. Saúl started receiving text messages sent from Elías's phone, saying, "You're next."

Saúl and Gloria took one last look at their house, their bakery, the bookshelves filled with books, their land. They walked across the bridge, leaving behind the country they loved, entering another from which as leftists they had always questioned seeking asylum. Living for months in a shelter for the homeless, piled on top of one another, unable to work, unable to do anything, having to accept help. Receiving asylum, getting a job in a supermarket with a salary that barely paid the rent on a tiny apartment for the family of five and Saúl's mother. Trying to make a paycheck last through the week. Losing your country.

"You plan out your life, you think it's going to go a certain way," Gloria says, smiling ironically, but without bitterness. "I remember when I was in my house, with our business and my three children, I thought, my life is so boring, nothing interesting ever happens. Just imagine."

Gloria says she doesn't like living in the United States, but one day she hopes to adequately thank all the people that welcomed them there. As long as there is life, she says, there is hope.

Gloria unclips her microphone, and before she leaves, José Luis gives her two books he brought along for Saúl, one by Eduardo Galeano and the other by José Saramago. Gloria thanks him and tells him how much her husband has enjoyed the other ones. He is even considering buying a bookcase.

We are in Carlos Spector's office in El Paso, a two-story building with walls adorned with Chicano artwork evoking the border. It has a warm, welcoming feel, in spite of the hundreds of manila folders with colored labels arranged in alphabetical order on shelves.

Today we're here to interview journalist Alejandro Hernández Pacheco. Carlos successfully handled his case for asylum. Alejandro just barely managed to get out alive.

José Luis sits down and assumes his role as the interviewer. Across from him, dressed casually, tall, with a solid build, large hands, and a ruddy complexion, sits Alejandro. He has coarse features, but a very gentle expression. He is timid at first, but once he gets comfortable, he speaks freely. José Luis hunches over a bit as the story unfolds, tilting his head to the right, gazing at his subject over his eyeglasses. He makes an effort to rephrase his academic modes of expression during interviews. All the little details in an interview help to get the story told.

Alejandro's father is a miner for the Peñoles mining company, the second largest in Mexico. For five years, Alejandro worked as a cameraman for the Telecable television network in Torreón before moving to Juárez. When he got there in 1997, the story of all the women being murdered started to make the news. He worked for the Televisión Azteca company, and then for the newspaper and Internet portal Milenio. In 2008, when things started getting tough in Torreón, he went back to work for Televisa, in an area of the city known as Laguna. Alejandro assures us that, from what he saw, the official number of reported murders during Felipe Calderón's presidency is much lower than the reality. He is the third person interviewed on this trip to tell us this. "Seeing so much death all around affects you at first," he says, "but then you get used to it . . . to the smell and everything."

Until it touches you. On July 26, 2010, Alejandro was kidnapped along with Héctor Gordoa, a producer for television journalist Denise Maerker's show *Punto de Partida* ("Jumping Off Point"), broadcast on the Televisa network, the largest television corporation in Mexico. They were working on an investigative story on the alleged complicity of prison officials with organized crime at the Centro de Rehabilitación Social in Gómez Palacio, Durango. The story implicated Margarita Rojas Rodríguez, the director of the prison at the time. On the drive back to Torreón, a vehicle cut them off and kidnapped them, along with another reporter who was released a short time later. The group that kidnapped them said that in exchange for their release, the Televisa network had to air a video linking officials with criminal activities of the narco gang Los Zetas. Televisa did not acquiesce, and on that day Maerker's show was not broadcast; after a brief explanation from Maerker, the screen stayed fixed on a logo.

"Televisa left us very vulnerable," Alejandro recalls. "Héctor and I joined hands and started to pray; we thought about our children." The two were blindfolded, tied up, and held in a house for two days. "There were dried bloodstains on the walls, and little scraps of hairy skin, teeth," says Alejandro. "When it was morning, I was surprised I hadn't been dismembered." He and Héctor were beaten, and didn't eat or sleep.

The kidnapping, which Alejandro attributes to a group affiliated with the Sinaloa cartel, lasted for five days. On the fifth day, for reasons he doesn't understand, they were both released. They immediately went to the federal police, who, it turned out, knew about the kidnapping already.

"They were waiting for us," Alejandro recalls, bitterly. "Genaro García Luna—the secretary of public security then, in Felipe Calderón's administration—put on a big show for the media, to announce our "rescue." They didn't even let us see our families. Without questioning us, without letting us see a doctor first, nothing, they put us on a plane and flew us to Mexico City for a press conference . . . Of course I was afraid to go back home, they had my name, they knew where I lived, and the whole time they told me they were going to kill me."

An official with Sitatyr, the union representing television and radio workers in Mexico, offered Alejandro temporary use of a house in Mexico City while Televisa resolved his situation. The company offered to relocate him to another city and to help pay for his housing costs. A week later they rescinded the offer.

Alejandro realized that neither the company nor the government was going to manage the situation. The public exhibition the government made of him, in fact, later helped Alejandro win his asylum case in the United States; that exposure, he argued, clearly demonstrated that the government lacked the most basic logistical knowledge necessary to protect his life. On August 21 he traveled to Chihuahua, and the next day he crossed the border, never to go back.

"We left behind everything, our families, our homes, our friends," he says. "To work so hard to get your home, only to leave it to those idiots . . ." His jaw is clenched with rage, as he tries to control himself. "They ransacked it, they took everything, the pipes, the window grates, everything."

When José Luis asks him what support he has received from international organizations, Alejandro smiles ruefully.

"I contacted Article 19, and Reporters Without Borders," he says. "I asked if there was some way they could give me some financial support while my asylum case was in process, because I couldn't work. They told me they didn't have the resources. They put out their little press releases about 'We support the reporter so-and-so' and that's about it."

Alejandro worked as a landscaper, he painted fences, he shined shoes. Like the other interviewees, he is tremendously grateful to all the people who did help him, some of whom he never even met. His was the second asylum case to be granted to a Mexican in the United States, under the grounds of persecution.

"We're peons, nothing more," he says. "The television network used us, the government used us, the narcos used us. We didn't matter to anybody. The new migration is journalists fleeing—not because they want to work here, but out of fear."

Kent and José Luis have an interesting rapport. They remind me of an old married couple who know each other's strengths and weaknesses perfectly. They get along well, and it's clear that their relationship is built on tolerance, respect, and affection.

We drive around the city in Kent's pickup truck, with a cabin that seats two comfortably in the front, and two more, uncomfortably, in the back. José Luis and I fight over who gets to sit in the back seat; I can better observe the academics' relationship from there, while he, old-fashioned, would feel badly if he were to travel more comfortably than a woman.

José Luis hails from the heart of Mexico City. His father has a business selling electrical equipment on Victoria Street, almost on the corner of Balderas. As a journalism student at the Autonomous University of Mexico in Aragón, he was awarded a Fulbright scholarship in 1988 to earn his master's degree at the University of Austin. Although he had originally planned on going back to Mexico, the financial crisis unleashed there in 1994, known as "the December mistake," helped convince him to continue his academic career in Texas.

José Luis is honest when he talks about his own migration experience. He knows he had a particularly privileged situation, a far cry from what hundreds of thousands of Latin American immigrants in the United States go through. "The immigration system in the U.S. is divided in two," he says. "It's designed to attract talent from outside, and in that sense it's easy to come here. But the other part forces people to migrate in very tough conditions, so they become cheap labor." Similarly, he says, "Austin is a city divided by race." He reflects on the racism in the academic world: the scholarships and grants that go through public and private networks made up of white, Anglo-Saxon professors, and the predominance of white ideology—"North American intellectual parochialism," as he puts it—in university systems that by their very nature should be diverse.

"We are giving these young people the knowledge and the history of their heritage," he says of the CSUN program. Without it, he says, "these students would be immersed in the monocultural education system of the United States, where coming from a different culture is not seen as an advantage, but a disadvantage . . . Our program reverses these roles: Do you know Spanish? You have opportunities to broaden your horizons. We want them to see journalism as a possible catalyst for change, like the black press has been. In that sense, these young people have a broader vision than many of their professors."

Kent, José Luis points out, is one of the few academics he knows who is sensitive to this diversity.

We travel down the highway surrounded by city lights, the ones in El Paso indistinguishable from the ones in Juárez. These two cities are sisters. None of the stories we have been hearing should have happened.

José Luis conducts all the Spanish-language interviews, and Kent handles those in English. On this trip, all the interviews have been in Spanish. José Luis stays calm, closely listening to the stories that tend to unfold in a matter-of-fact way for the first hour, but by the third hour have built to a soul-crushing intensity. It's as if the speaker's pain permeates the very air around us. When we breathe it in, it settles deep in our bones; by the evening our bones ache, as if we have just run a marathon.

I am struck by how Kent manages to get through the long interviews in a language he doesn't speak, so good-naturedly. When I comment on this, he reminds me that his wife is Mexican, and that he is used to being in this situation during all of their family gatherings. Still, it is clear that although Kent may not understand the words, he understands what is going on, especially at the most painful moments. I observe how he reacts in a far less visceral way than José Luis, as if he was accustomed to confronting pain. *It must be because he's a gringo,* I think to myself one afternoon.

A few weeks after our trip, we are sitting in Kent's office at the Institute of Arts and Media at CSUN, a large room with black-and-white photographs adorning the walls, including a striking image of Martin Luther King Jr., the Reverend Ralph Abernathy, and Sammy Davis Jr. at a civil rights march in Los Angeles. Kent tells me about some events in his life as if they had happened to someone else, making an effort to remember the details, giving me not particularly long answers: in 1965 he joined the U.S. Marines, and spent two and a half years in Waukegan, Illinois, working in a medical laboratory at a navy hospital with 800 beds. This was during the war in Vietnam—he is emphatic on this point: not *the* Vietnam war, but the war *in* Vietnam. In 1968, the marines sent him to the front lines.

All of Kent's sixty-seven years are visible in his clear blue eyes. I have known him for several weeks now; we spent five days together in El Paso–Juárez listening to horrific stories. But as we talk on this day, it's the first time I see the mark of pain that settled deep inside him after he was "not in the rice paddies, but up in the mountains, in the jungle, up, down, 'looking for' the enemy." He describes tending to the wounded flown in on helicopters, bleeding, missing limbs, with their guts hanging out. He describes watching a friend die on the operating table.

"I know people who are overwhelmed with guilt; it's a natural reaction for people who come back," he says. "You see people in the States like nothing happened, going shopping, not knowing about what's happening in Iraq or in Afghanistan, sending their kids to Sunday school and to soccer practice, not realizing they are part of a machine that prepares them to kill people ... [Military service] is the closest thing to a slave a white person can be in this country. And now I accept that it was part of my life, even that it's something that has had a role in my emotional life as an adult. Maybe that's why some people think I'm detached. But you learn to live with it."

# 9

## Impunity

Sandra Rodríguez is sitting at the edge of the bed. We are in the same bedroom where José Luis interviewed Gloria three days before. Sandra lives in Juárez, but she has come to El Paso to continue a conversation with José Luis and Kent, which began on July 29 the year before.

An experienced journalist, at forty Sandra is tall and slender, with long, wavy hair, a penetrating gaze, and a measured smile, marked by the bloodshed of the Calderón years. She grew up in the city of Chihuahua. In 1993, when she was nineteen, she moved to Juárez to go to school and began working at the newspaper *El Diario de Juárez*, where she stayed for four years. After a stint working for other news outlets in other cities, she returned to *El Diario* in 2003. For eight years her job was to report on everything that happened in Juárez, at a time when everything started happening in Juárez.

"A lot of people in 2007 knew there was going to be a battle [between crime syndicates] for the city," Sandra told José Luis in her first interview. "But in January [of 2008] I do remember a series of murders, and among those there were several that didn't have any signs of organized crime, but you noticed them because it was so apparent: there were a lot of murders, a lot . . . And by January 21, when they fired on the police, it was very clear: this is going to be very heavy. I remember I wrote a story to close the month, the most violent in years—forty-three killed."

Sandra's perception of that era coincides with Charles Bowden's, the American journalist who Kent and José Luis invited to CSUN. In his book *Murder City*, Bowden provided an analysis of the culture of violence in Juárez, its origins, and the toll it took on both sides of the border. In one passage, Bowden describes how, while gathering documentation for a story, he followed the unstoppable wave of growing violence in the city.

At first, it is simply a clerical task. Read the papers and put down the names, if given, and the time of death. Then the volume grows, and the reports get sketchy. People disappear, and their fates never get reported. Nor are there any real numbers on the kidnapped since families hardly ever report such events, because they are afraid of being murdered. Then, the killings per day get larger, the reporters more and more threatened. By June 2008, the city cannot handle its own dead and starts giving corpses wholesale to medical schools or tossing bodies into common graves . . . By the end of 2008, the monthly totals [of people killed] reached beyond two hundred. By summer 2009, more than three hundred murders in a month becomes normal in Juárez.[1]

In Bowden's almost obsessive reporting, in one article after another, the story of escalating violence is told. On

January 3, a man is killed in his car. On January 5, a homeless man was found with his head bashed in by a rock. On
January 12, the newspaper reports sixteen murders have
been committed so far that month. On January 24, the
district attorney is trying to identify the murderer of a young
girl. On January 25, Catholic leaders pray for an end to the
violence. On January 27, a handwritten sign is found on a
street with the names of four municipal Secretary of Public
Security agents who had recently been killed, and another
seventeen agents, still alive, with the message: "to the non-
believers." On January 28, an El Paso newspaper quoted
Bowden: "The United States government has not stopped
drug trafficking to the interior of the country, and this has
caused a rise in violence in Mexico, especially along the
border."

Sandra understands this phenomenon—the violence in
Juárez, something many are still struggling to explain—better
than almost anyone. It is not just about the war on
narcotrafficking, and it's not a specific period in time with a
clear beginning and end. It has to do with at least two decades
when Juárez became a social laboratory, and several factors
converged: the agricultural sector ceased to be a main source
of income, with industrialization and factories taking its place
as a result of the North American Free Trade Agreement
(NAFTA); the demographic growth that took place resulting
from the rise in industry, without adequate urban planning to
support that growth; and the increase in narcotrafficking cartel
activities, among other things.

In an effort to make sense of these factors, Sandra wrote
her first book, *La Fábrica del Crimen*. Starting with the story
of León, a sixteen-year-old boy who killed his parents and

sister and set their bodies on fire, Sandra analyzed recent events in Juárez and the cultural normalization of violence there. The key factor: impunity.

Traveling there by plane, it's easy to make out Juárez on the ground below. Juárez is a gray splotch dotted here and there with green, in the middle of a vast brownish-orange desert. In this sandy expanse that goes on for miles—and which around El Paso–Juárez becomes a jumble of desert, houses, factories, mountains, factories, houses, more desert—a clear line delineates the two countries. On a clear day, the four border bridges connecting the two cities look like stitches trying to close a wound. A mountain to the west bears a message in enormous white letters: "Ciudad Juárez. La Biblia es la verdad. Leéla." ("Juárez City. The Bible is the truth. Read it.") This is, of course, on the Mexican side.

Violence in Juárez has been growing since 1993. In 1997 there were 250 killings in the city, most of them after the death of drug kingpin Amado Carrillo Fuentes, known as "The Lord of the Sky," who became head of the Juárez cartel in 1993 after his predecessor, former federal police commander Rafael Aguilar, was assassinated.

The city experienced a population explosion and economic growth during those years. Once a mid-size city, it became the capital of Mexico's burgeoning factory industry in the 1990s. Dozens of multinational corporations subcontracted to other companies, which sent buses with recruiters down to states in Southern Mexico, bringing back tens of thousands of workers who joined the labor force and bustling scene on the border, at a rate of almost 100,000 newcomers a year.[2] The population grew at rates never before registered in any other part of Mexico. Paradoxically, Juárez became an employment "paradise" in the decade when thousands of rural jobs were lost, as a result of competition from government-subsidized U.S. agriculture after NAFTA went into full effect in 1994. This new reality seemed like a win-win: factories generated jobs for Mexicans, and the multinational corporations had an attractive business model. While factory jobs in the United States paid $200 per week, salaries for employees in Mexico were just $60 per week. For millions in Mexico, factory work and narcotrafficking became the only employment options.

Juárez is the capital of both industries, although the latter is not openly discussed. In official communications the government deliberately positioned the factories as the engine that would grow the national economy. With attractive financial incentives and favorable tariffs for investors, every part needed for assembling cars was produced in the plants and factories built in Juárez. These factories needed workers, and the workers themselves meant dynamic growth for the local economy: this new population required housing, transportation, food, schools, entertainment, and means of communication, and these needs represented a major opportunity for those who wanted to invest in the region. As Sandra writes in her book,

> The money poured in, and you could see it in the continuous construction of warehouses, shopping centers, and, especially in the southwest, housing developments with thousands of homes for the factory workers. And there were thousands of cars on the streets, new and older models, and just about anyone could buy one because the United States was getting rid of millions of used ones. On top of

that, we all went out almost every night to dozens of packed bars and restaurants. There were still even some North American tourists.[3]

But stark signs of inequality also emerged across the city along with the heady rise of industrial production and commercial growth, an unplanned surge in population, and narcotrafficking. Half a million people suddenly found themselves living in hastily constructed slums at the foot of the mountains emblazoned with a message promising the Bible as their salvation. It would take years for basic services like running water and electricity and a sewage system to arrive. Large tracts of land filled with sand, trash, and leftover debris from housing construction separated this area from the other side, the southwest neighborhoods, "like islands in a sea of desolation and waste." The long walk to work in the factories from one side of the city to the other became a challenge, and very soon posed a real danger.

On top of the physical evidence that the new wave of economic growth in Juárez was not benefiting the residents of the city came the spiraling violence reflecting social and political imbalances. Between 1993 and 1997, the bodies of over 150 murdered women were dumped throughout the city and in desert land surrounding it. This wave of violence was widely covered in the local media, inciting feminist groups to action. In 1997 the story was picked up by national and then international media, and the victims became known as "las muertas de Juárez" (the dead women of Juárez).

"The brutality with which they had been killed," Sandra wrote, "and the way their bodies were found . . . revealed the existence of a contempt for human life, the implications and lessons of which we as a society have yet to understand."

At this time the "levantón," or "pick-up," arose in the Juárez popular consciousness: kidnapping a person "at gunpoint, almost in silence" from their home, or as they left work, or as they were simply out walking the streets. That was how criminal groups settled scores.

By 1997, narcotrafficker Amado Carrillo controlled the region. He lived up to his nickname, "Lord of the Sky," which he had earned thanks to the fleet of aircraft at his disposal for transporting massive quantities of illicit drugs from Colombia. It was common knowledge that the drug cartel enjoyed the protection of the Mexican army, the police, officials from all levels of government, and politicians from all parties. The city therefore stayed silent, and the men who had been "picked up" were linked in public discourse to the criminal activities of these groups and "buried in the communal grave of suspicion." These men had disappeared because they had made a "misstep." But no logical explanation existed for the women's killings.

Observing the city's dizzying transformation as both a resident and reporter, Sandra Rodríguez noted,

> The physical characteristics of the city were more than favorable for someone to commit a crime. Just seeing all the big empty spaces all over the place was enough to understand how easy it would be to be the victim of an attack without anyone being able to help, or even hear you scream.[4]

In July 1997, Amado Carrillo died during a plastic surgery procedure in Mexico City. His death unleashed a war for territory between organized crime groups: assassinations took place in broad daylight and deaths multiplied, with no motive supplied for the murders. Sandra describes this period during her second interview with José Luis in El Paso. She seems tense. A few months earlier, she resigned from *El Diario*, and she seems to be settling accounts. "All the elements that fed the violence that we lived through are still there: corruption, impunity, trafficking, business, and permissiveness," she says.

Sandra describes how the judicial reform announced in 2004 and put into effect in 2008, which aimed to eliminate excessive bureaucracy and corruption in the Mexican criminal justice system, resulted in stripping the system down in Juárez to an apparatus of police, expert witnesses, and Public Ministry agents incapable of presenting evidence that would implicate those likely responsible for crimes. By 2010, evidence was presented in only three of every hundred murder cases. Expert witnesses continue to work: recording the time the victim was found, a description of the body's position, autopsy data, entry and exit points of bullets, a description of each wound, sometimes amounting to hundreds of gunshots. But in the vast majority of cases, no further clues are sought. No witnesses are found and questioned beyond the victim's family members, and that is almost always to get a single piece of information: What did the victim do for work? If there is any indication that the victim may have had direct or indirect contact with narcotrafficking, the investigation will most likely try to establish which criminal group could be implicated in the matter. And that is the end of the investigation, which concludes that the killing was the result of drug gang warfare.

José Luis and Sandra talk about the hundreds of stories she told as a journalist in those years, some of which appeared in her book, and how they helped her to understand the causes and consequences of impunity. Its local manifestations in Juárez are, she says, evident throughout the country. "Pay close attention to the justice system," she warns, "because a country that does not punish . . . crime will never be able to stop it."

# 10

# Seeking Justice from the Other Side

Nitza Paola Alvarado Espinoza was kidnapped on December 29, 2009. She and her two cousins José Angel and Rocío Irene were taken away in military vehicles. The cousins were detained by elements of the Mexican National Secretary of Defense (SEDENA)—the Mexican army—in the municipality of Ejido Benito Juárez Buenaventura. The three all worked in factories in Juárez, just across the border from El Paso, Texas. Nitza and José were taken together, while Rocío was kidnapped in a separate incident. The military personnel did not present an order of arrest for any of them. The cousins' whereabouts are unknown to this day.

Nitza Paola had three daughters, twins Mitzi and Nitza, who were thirteen at the time, and Deisy, who was eleven years old. The last time the Alvarado sisters saw their mother was the morning of December 29.

I met the Alvarado sisters in early August 2014, in El Paso. They had been living there for less than a year. In the five years since their mother and cousins had disappeared, the rest of the family had been moving around from city to city within Mexico, trying to escape the harassment and intimidation they had been subjected to when they tried to seek justice for the disappearances. In the end, they all came to the United States to apply for political asylum. Carlos Spector took their case.

The Alvarado sisters are pure sweetness. Slender, with long brown hair and round childlike smiles, the three girls carry themselves with a cheerful, easy grace. But Mitzi and Nitza, high-school seniors at eighteen, and Deisy, sixteen, a sophomore, all have a certain indelible sadness in their eyes even when they smile—a sadness I've noticed in every person I've talked to who has lost a loved one to violence. The Alvarado girls, as they are called by the activist groups that have become part of their daily lives, first in Mexico and now the United States, have spent a third of their young lives demanding an investigation into their mother's disappearance.

The Alvarado girls used to live in Juárez with their mother, Nitza Paola, and their maternal grandparents. In late December 2009, they all traveled to a nearby town, Ejido Benito Juárez, to spend the holidays with relatives. They celebrated Christmas and were preparing to ring in the new year when what Nitza calls "my family's tragedy" took place. On December 29, Nitza Paola's cousin José Angel arrived and asked her to go with him to his wife's house. As they drove up to the house, a Mexican army commando intercepted them, took them into custody, and drove off. Witnesses described a dozen military troops getting out of their trucks, beating the cousins, and taking them away— "los levantaron."

"When they started to take them away our relatives tried to get involved, they asked why they were taking them, but they told them to get down on the ground," Nitza describes in the flat tone of someone who has had to tell this story many times, and each time tries not to think too hard about what she is actually saying. "They made the children go inside and they started beating José Angel's family." Outside, the heat of the Texas summer rises, but we are talking in the cool, comfortable library in the Spectors' home. The Alvarado girls have lived with Carlos, his wife Sandra, and their daughter Alejandra for the past nine months.

Once the commando unit had driven off with the two cousins, bystanders tried to drive after them, but the military trucks sped through back roads and lost them. They found out that military personnel had carried out a similar operation with Rosa Irene, another cousin of Nitza Paola's, locking her children in the bathroom, pulling her baby daughter from her arms, and taking her away.

Just as with all families who have had to confront the disappearance of one of their own, they were faced not just with the raw pain of loss but also with the sheer ineptitude of Mexican bureaucracy and the indifference, or open complicity, of the authorities responsible for meting out justice. On December 30, Nitza Paola's sister María Jesús Alvarado drove to the city of Casas Grandes, where, according to declarations by witnesses to the kidnapping, the cousins had been driven and where they had spent the night of December 29 at the 35th Infantry Battalion base. Military personnel told her that neither the cousins nor the truck had been there, though she found out later that the latter had been parked behind the building during her visit.

This was when Joint Operation Chihuahua was taking place, Mitzi says, picking up her sister's story. The military kidnapped and tortured people but brought them back two or three days later. "We thought it would be the same thing with my family, they would show up again a few days later." The family filed one complaint after another with the federal attorney general. At one point, María de Jesús and José Angel's mother overheard two employees discussing the Alvarado family and implying that something had happened to one of them. When the employees realized that family members were listening to them, they stopped talking. Piece by piece, the family was gathering clues and signs of hope in their search.

On February 3, 2010, thirty-five days after the disappearance, Nitza Paola's best friend told the family that Nitza had called her from a number in Mexico City. According to the friend's account, Nitza told her that she did not know where she was, but pleaded that they keep searching for her. The family filed another complaint with the attorney general, asking the government to investigate the phone call, which turned out to have come from the women's prison in Santa Martha Acatitla, in Mexico City. "But the government said it wasn't her," Mitzi says. "They said someone from inside was trying to extort us, and they closed all lines of investigation."

As soon as the family understood the magnitude of the kidnapping, they set up a network of relatives to protect Nitza, Mitzi, and Deisy. The girls traveled to the city of Cuernavaca in the state of Morelos in central Mexico first. After spending their entire lives as part of an extended nuclear family, life in Cuernavaca with only their grandmother meant losing touch with everything they had known up until that point. They did not talk on the phone for fear that it had been tapped. They missed their aunt María de Jesús, who had filed the complaints with the attorney general and therefore cut off all contact with the girls to avoid putting them in any danger. They met up with her in Mexico City on the following May 10, when Mother's Day is celebrated in Mexico. They could only see her for thirty minutes. And the harassment from the government did not stop: federal and municipal authorities surrounded their family home in Benito Juárez, where the kidnapping had taken place, several times, in an apparent show of intimidation.

The family could tell how hard the situation was on the girls, so they decided to move to the city of Hermosillo, in Sonora state, to be together. At the same time, at the suggestion of activist groups working on their behalf, María de Jesús began to bring the girls with her to meetings in order to involve them in the search and show them why the process was taking so long. Soon activist groups in Chihuahua and some media outlets started talking about the case. The story of three sisters left without a mother, represented by the lawyer Luz "Lucha" Castro, founder of the Women's Human Rights Center, was bound to attract attention. The case helped launch a statewide movement for the disappeared, led by Castro and Alma Gómez Camino.

"We weren't scared," Nitza tells me later, calm and composed. "We were happy to go in with the necessary strength to seek justice and truth. Not only for my family, but for the other people who had disappeared."

On May 10, 2011, the Alvarado sisters played a prominent role in honoring all the mothers who had disappeared. During an event organized by a human rights organization in Mexico City, their lawyer Luz Castro decided that Mitzi and Nitza would read the names of all the disappeared in the state of Chihuahua. Nitza still gets emotional when she talks about it.

"It was very powerful to us, to say all the names and the people answered back, 'Here!'" she says. "When that part ended we were very emotional, but then the media came up to us and attacked us with questions and more questions: 'If your mother was here, what would you say to her? If you were spending Mother's Day with her, what present would you give her?' What stupid questions! Why would they ask us that? We're not with our mom; we're searching for her! How am I going to think about what present I would give her? The only thing I want is to have her with me. When our lawyer [Lucha Castro] realized what was going on, she stopped the interviews. We weren't prepared; it was really hard for us."

A few weeks later they began family and individual therapy. After just a few months the change was apparent. The girls began going to meetings held by organizations of families of the disappeared more often, actively participating more each time.

On May 10, 2012, their third Mother's Day without their mother, the girls met with members of Hijos por la Identidad y la Justicia contra el Olvido y el Silencio (HIJOS) Mexico, the Mexican chapter of the organization founded in Argentina by children of the disappeared and political prisoners, to demand justice and make sure that their parents are not forgotten by history.

"They helped us a lot," Nitza says. "They have been searching for their parents for years—they motivated us, and gave us strength."

After living in Sonora for two years, the family decided to move back to Chihuahua. All eleven people—María de Jesús and her husband, their four children, the three Alvarado sisters, and their maternal grandparents—had been surviving on their uncle's income. María de Jesús started to work part-time, but she was also taking care of the seven children and working on her sister's case. Moving back to Chihuahua and living closer to their extended family there seemed likely to make things easier for everybody. But there, the harassment only increased. One of José Angel's brothers was run over, and his house was broken into and ransacked. Some people appeared in town and menaced the family members.

Thanks to the tireless efforts of the family and supporting organizations, the Alvarado case reached the Inter-American Court of Human Rights. The Secretary of Defense acknowledged that the army was involved in the disappearances. But "instead of offering us protection, they just harassed us," Mitzi says. "We couldn't go out. We didn't feel comfortable at school." After the intimidating phone calls started—"we heard men and women screaming, a chain saw, that kind of thing," Mitzi says—the entire family decided to apply for asylum in the United States.

The Alvarado family presented themselves at one of the bridges connecting Juárez with El Paso on September 3, 2013.

Walking over the bridge from the Mexican side to the U.S. side can be intimidating. As you walk, your mind races with questions immigration agents might ask you, and if you are seeking asylum, the rest of your life could depend on how you answer those questions. An incorrect answer or a poorly presented argument could slam the door shut on your ability to live. María de Jesús spoke for the group, showing the immigration agent the pages of legal documents that had been prepared under the guidance of Lucha Castro and Carlos Spector. "They took our pictures, fingerprints," Mitzi remembers. "They asked a lot of questions and tried to discourage us."

"They kept us there for a long time," Nitza adds, her anxiety rising at the memory. "They started to talk to us one at a time, asking us who we were. They put us in some rooms and my sisters and I were there for hours and hours, for two days and a night." While their aunt and grandparents were released to begin their asylum petition process after establishing credible fear, the girls were kept in detention because they were "unaccompanied children"—their legal guardian being their mother. Then they were transferred to a shelter for minors in Phoenix, Arizona—the first time they had ever been on a plane.

The Hacienda del Sol youth shelter, part of the Southwest Key system, is one of 637 centers around the country that ICE uses to transfer detainees. Although 40 percent of those detained by ICE are from Mexico,[1] in that particular center only 6 percent of arrivals between 2013 and 2015 were Mexican, with 64 percent from Guatemala, 20 percent from Honduras, 6 percent from El Salvador and 3 percent from Romania. According to official data, the average length of a stay at the youth shelter is fifty-three days.

"They treated us well," Nitza acknowledges. Mitzi later tells me about some of the experiences the kids at the shelter had shared with her: sexual abuse in the family, physical abuse, gang recruitment. "A lot of the kids didn't even know what a bathroom was, or how you make a bed . . . They divided us into groups A through D, from the most educated down to the ones who couldn't even write. They were learning there. There were some who didn't even speak Spanish; they had their own dialects and we couldn't understand them. It was really hard, because they had to learn Spanish and English."

After spending two months in the youth shelter, the sisters got the good news that their aunt María de Jesús had been named their legal guardian, and they could be released. Now their legal process would begin, during which they could remain in the United States. For the time being, the threats, Juárez, and Mexico were behind them.

I asked the girls to tell me about the last memory they have of Juárez. Nitza tells me she remembers her life with her mom, at home. It's the first time in the conversation when it seems she may be overcome by tears.

"For me, the last memory I have of Juárez is my house with my family," Mitzi says. "It's so sad because we had to abandon the house, and it's all still there, my mom's clothes, her bedroom, just like when we left. Leaving the house behind made us really sad too."

Nitza says, perhaps more to herself than to me, that her mother will come back someday.

How do you start a new life, if the wounds of the old life have not healed? Impunity hurts, even from exile. Talking about this pain can be not only an effective method of counteracting it, but also a legal strategy. The case of the Alvarado girls is one of the best examples of this.

In the human rights field, especially in the area focusing on those disappeared by violence, the Alvarado case has become iconic for two reasons. First, the compelling story of three young girls denouncing abuses perpetrated by federal and local authorities against their mother has propelled the case into the media both nationally and internationally. On November 29, 2013, the *New York Times* ran a story originally published in the *Texas Tribune*, directly blaming the Mexican army for Nitza Paola's disappearance: "Daughters Look for a Mother Lost to the Mexican Military." Second, the Alvarado case was the first case of violence in Mexico to reach the Inter-American Court of Human Rights.

Carlos Spector points out that the increased harassment of the Alvarado family following the court's ruling is part of a general strategy of repression that focuses on human rights activists and others of the most vocal citizens. "The case was first presented to the Inter-American Commission on Human Rights, implicating Colonel Elfego José Luján Ruiz in Nitza Paola's disappearance, as a result of investigations performed by the organizations presenting the case," Spector explains. "Then it went on to the Court, which accepted the case and presented it to the media on August 13, 2013, condemning the Mexican government for its incompetence or lack of interest, and the army for not cooperating in resolving the case. And what we saw was the army responded by doubling down on its harassment of the Alvarado Espinosa family, surrounding the house with fifty soldiers from the federal, state, and municipal police. Obviously, at that moment the family said 'we can't take it anymore.' If the response to international criticism is increased harassment, they didn't have any other choice. Then they fled, and that's when we took the case. The way it developed is emblematic because it's a continuation of the repression that started in 2008, identifying and focusing on the human rights activists and on people who make 'noise.' 'It's a strategy consistent with the PRI's return to federal power in 2012, using old tactics," he says. "The government is effectively saying, "If this is the most symbolic case in the country, we're going to shut them up and show that making noise is not going to help them.'"

We are in Carlos's living room. The Alvarado girls are here too, and their grandmother, who is living in Odessa, Texas, has come over to visit. Carlos speaks admiringly of the girls. He is impressed with how well they have managed to go on with their lives and continue the search for their mother, demanding justice and involving others. He is also impressed by their generosity. But it has been the Spectors' generosity that has given the girls some stability. As soon as the girls' aunt María de Jesús, her husband, and their grandparents were released from detention, the harsh reality of life in the United States hit them: the language barrier, the absence of family and friends, the difficulty of finding a well-paying job, and the high cost of living in dollars. When María was granted guardianship of the girls two months later and they were sent to live with her, it was clear that their financial situation would be even more precarious. The Spectors decided to support the family by letting the girls live with them and attend school in El Paso.

"We had never done anything like that before," Carlos says. "I am a very private person . . . But the Alvarado Espinosa family is so unique, with such a historic case. These girls are so brave, so charismatic . . . When I met them, they were fifteen and seventeen, and already veterans of the

Mexican social movement. They had already participated in sit-ins in Chihuahua to occupy the Municipal Palace. It is amazing what the children of the disappeared in Mexico have done and what they have achieved. For me, the girls represent courage, and at the same time they remind us of the Mexican tradition of social struggle. They are here to show the people of the United States that the idea that the Mexican people are passively watching what's going on in Mexico with their arms crossed is totally false—it's just the opposite."

"They have been our angels since we got here," Mitzi tells me that afternoon, talking about the Spector family. "We are so grateful to them," she says, and beams the brightest smile of the whole day.

Deisy is the most reserved of the three Alvarado sisters. She is two years younger than her sisters, although only one year behind them in school. She talks less than the twins, and a bit faster. She speaks emphatically but never raises her voice. Mitzi says that after their mother disappeared, Deisy had the hardest time expressing her feelings. She would just cry, and couldn't talk about how she felt. Her sisters would hug her and try to get her to tell them what she was thinking, and then they would all end up crying together.

Surprisingly, when their new lives began in El Paso, Deisy was the one who settled in the fastest. On top of the language barrier, the twins had no friends in school and did not understand the social dynamics there. Most of their relatives were still in Mexico. But there are many Mexican students in Deisy's school, since, as is common in cities along the border, some live on the Mexican side and cross north during the week to attend school in the United States. She likes her teachers. Despite some difficulty adjusting to the food (chicken potpie, for example), she's been able to find the positives in their new life.

"They ask us to tell them our story, and many people are shocked, because they don't think things like that really happen. Things that happen in Mexico get covered in the news, but they don't really believe it can be true. When they hear our story, they give us all their support. A lot of people think as soon as you get to the U.S. you're free and you don't have to do anything anymore, but at least for us we're still searching for my mom, and we're not going to stop until we find her. We're still fighting from here," she says. "We're still protesting, marching, pressuring the government. So that in Mexico and the United States, they find out what happened to them."

Continuing the fight is what gives them strength to face everything else, Nitza says, and to handle all the daily challenges of life in the United States.

"We can't get all upset over school, or learning a new language, if we know we have a much more important fight with the government," she says firmly, shaking her head.

The question of justice riles Mitzi. She knows the man responsible for her mother's kidnapping, Colonel Luján Ruiz, is in prison in Mexico City, "but not for what he did to my family, for other crimes," she says, indignant. "We're living for ourselves, but also in case our mom comes back some day, she'll see that we kept going, we went ahead with our lives."

Since Mitzi will graduate from high school soon, I ask her where she sees herself in ten years.

"Successful," she replies right away. "Finishing school. I want to go to law school, probably because of what we've been through."

Nitza has been similarly inspired by the legal profession. "I want to be like Carlos, and do immigration. I want to help people who have gone through things like we have."

At the end of the afternoon, I ask the Alvarado sisters to tell me in one word how they feel about Mexico, and the United States. The three all describe Mexico as "violence." For the United States, they say "peace," "calm," and "security."

Before leaving, I mention to Carlos how passionately the three Alvarado girls spoke about wanting to keep fighting for justice from this side of the border. Their approach to this fight, he says, is the most effective: pressuring the Mexican community from abroad.

"They had never even left Juárez before, and now they've given major presentations in Houston, San Antonio, and Austin; their story was in the *New York Times*," he says. "They're on the cover of international reports on the disappeared. They lost two years of school, but now they're in high school and learning English, because they want to be lawyers." Growing emotional, Carlos pauses. "They represent the very best of Mexico. The Alvarado girls are a national treasure that Mexico has thrown in the trash."

# Part Four
# Here We Are

# 11
## Back to Life

Life in Fabens unfolds at its own pace. Heading east on Interstate 10, El Paso's urban rhythms, smooth paved streets, and diverse architectural styles—Tudor Revival, Classical Revival, Queen Anne, Colonial Revival—give way to a calm, quiet panorama of rural desert, with simple homes and buildings typical of far-western Texas. The air feels heavier, with a slightly misty look from the fine desert dust. Radio stations fade in and out.

The dust, which rises up into clouds as you drive along Fabens's dirt roads, is what I remember most viscerally when I think about my visits to the *trailas* here. The stories of exiles rebuilding their lives in Texas play out against a backdrop of desert silence.

Martín Huéramo has invited me into his home for another conversation. Sitting at his dining room table, he tells me more about leaving Guadalupe, coming to Fabens and finding Saúl there, and what it's been like trying to start a new life. Martín's trailer home, in better condition than Saúl's, has relatively new furniture, with photos of his children displayed throughout. Just like Fabens itself, Martín is in no rush. It is January 2014 and cold, so before we sit down, he makes sure that his electric heater is working and makes coffee. He tells me about the repairs and home improvements he and his wife have made, pointing to the walls, the floor, the windows. He can't help but also talk about the obstacles he has encountered in the four years he has lived here. Leaving one's home means dying a little, and coming back to life is not easy.

Martín ran into his first challenge when he had to fill out some forms for the first time. He did not understand them since they were in English. He realized that aside from having to ask someone else what the form said, he also had to trust somebody else to tell him exactly what to write, and where. Martín asked several people about the same form, "to see if they were telling me the truth." Then came the second blow: he could not work in the U.S. without a Social Security number, because it was against the law. But he had to support his family somehow. And he could not drive without a license, but in a place like Fabens, not having a car basically meant you couldn't get a job, especially in Martín's line of work. So, after years of doing everything the right way, trying to be a good citizen, he found himself in a serious dilemma.

"Here, everything is against the law. You can't do a lot of things, but you have to do them out of necessity," he says, taking a sip of coffee.

Like the others, Martín asked about how the asylum process worked as soon as he arrived. He had been a city councilman in Guadalupe, in addition to his construction work, and had been involved in social activism and politics in Guadalupe for many years. He and members of the Reyes family were militant members of the leftist Revolutionary Democratic Party (PRD) together. Martín was secretary of Guadalupe's local PRD branch when Eleazar Reyes, the eldest brother in the Reyes family, was its president. When Eleazar died, Martín served as interim president. Martín worked with Saúl and Josefina Reyes to devise a strategy to defeat the conservative National Action Party (PAN), which was riding high after the electoral triumph in 2000 of President Vicente Fox, the first PAN president of Mexico after seventy-one years of PRI administrations. The PRI activists saw their allies fall in a spiral of resistance, threats, and death. In 2008, the tension reached a boiling point: police officers were assassinated, and shots fired on the municipal presidential building. One day, three human heads appeared in front of the building. Martín was approached by a man who rattled off a list of construction jobs performed by Martín in recent months, and how much he had charged for each one. "You have nice children; take that money and get out of here," he said.

"We wanted to support [President] Calderón but we weren't given any tools," Martín explains, seemingly to justify his departure from Mexico. He returns over and over again to this part of the story. After the municipal president and then two city council members were killed, Martín reluctantly left the country at the urging of his friends and brought his family to El Paso. Lacking the funds to buy land or even rent, he accepted the offer of a woman he knew from Guadalupe to let him live in a mobile home, in poor condition. In exchange, he points out emphatically, he made many repairs and improvements to the home. He and his family lived there for six months.

"I figured in around six months, things were going to change in Mexico. I even thought, the day Calderón leaves office, things are going to change. But then it was 2010 and they killed Josefina Reyes, and Rubén, and other colleagues, and I saw that things were not going to stop."[1]

Martín began to consider applying for asylum. Several of the lawyers he consulted asked him why he didn't just move to another state in the central or southern part of Mexico, instead of coming to the United States. Martín realized that people in the United States really had no idea what things were like in Mexico. He, as a councilman, had not had the support of the Chihuahua state government or the federal government. He could count on even less support in any other state.

"Moving to central Mexico meant taking my children there so they could be big criminals someday," Martín says. "White-collar criminals if they're educated, or if not, common street thugs. This is what I want the United States to understand, the magnitude of the problem the Mexican government has created. Here in the United States, they allow people to own guns and defend their homes, their property . . . In Mexico the Secretary of National Defense regulates arms, but . . . even the municipal police have obsolete weapons, while the criminals have much more modern weapons they get smuggled in, and the government knows this. You can't win."

Then Martín reconnected with Saúl, who told him about Carlos Spector. Martín presented his case to him, and Carlos said he might be able to help.

Four years later, and in spite of everything, the Huéramo family has managed to settle in. Martín's children have had their ups and downs, but they have adjusted to school. Martín proudly shows me a photo of his eldest son, who plays on an American football team. Still, Martín hopes that his sons will not always live "in a country that is not theirs," although it will most likely be a long time before they can return. It pains Martín to be on this side of the border. "No one comes here wanting to stay," he says, as if this were a universal truth. "Here you have to learn how to live."

Later in our conversation, Martín confides that one of the reasons he has stayed in Fabens is because he wants to return to Mexico. Many people he knew from Guadalupe have gone to Oklahoma to find a better place for their families. He doesn't believe that leaving for another state is the answer. He can die in peace, he says, only when he has left his children in their motherland or at least obtained asylum for them. Of course that wouldn't be the same as being in their own country, but in the end that is what they can do for now. By this point in our talk, Martín's eyes have filled with tears.

"Now I know, being born on this planet does not guarantee you can live freely." A tear runs down his cheek. "I believe exile is something human beings are obligated to live . . . It's hard to accept because you want to adapt to this world, and you realize you are not of this world."

Carlos Spector's office has changed almost as much as he has over the last few years. The façade of the little two-story building, painted gray, on the north side of the highway that splits El Paso in two, has stayed the same, but the files inside have multiplied and filled the building. One of the oldest and fattest case files is that of Cipriana Jurado, the first Mexican human rights defender who, under Carlos's representation, was granted political asylum in the United States.

Cipriana, a single mother of two children, went to Juárez to work in a factory when she was just thirteen years old. There, she founded the Center for Investigation and Worker Solidarity, which operated out of her home with the help of volunteers to fight for workers' rights, and to denounce and investigate the murders of women in the city. Cipriana was a lifelong friend of Josefina Reyes, Saúl's sister. In 2007, when the first troops sent by Felipe Calderón started arriving in Juárez, Josefina and Cipriana organized public protests to denounce the disappearances, torture, and murder of local residents. Neighbors and acquaintances relied on them for help.

Although attempts had been made to intimidate Cipriana before, the direct attacks started in 2009, after she denounced the torture and murder of a fellow activist. There were several break-in attempts at her house, files were stolen from her office, and her son, then nineteen, was followed and threatened. Several human rights groups, including Amnesty International, recommended that she apply for political asylum in the United States.

Just like Martín, Saúl, and most others who have had to make this difficult decision, Cipriana did not want to leave Mexico. She felt responsible for the people who worked with her and an obligation to continue pressuring the government to investigate hundreds of murders and disappearances. But then, Josefina Reyes's son was killed. Cipriana went to the funeral; looking at the coffin that held his young body, she knew her own son could be next. In 2010, an organization in Chicago invited her to give a presentation on violence in Juárez. She went with her children, and when her visa expired in December, she did not return to Mexico. A Presbyterian church in New Mexico gave her financial assistance and a place to live as she began the process of applying for asylum.

"When we left Mexico, the idea was to stay in Chicago for just a few months," Cipriana tells me in a phone conversation from her home in Santa Fe. She has lived there for four years with her son, now twenty-two, and her daughter, eleven. "But things got worse, and like a lot of people, I thought if you apply for asylum, you'd never be able to go back to Mexico ever." She got in touch with Carlos Spector, whom she knew from his work with migrants in El Paso. Carlos and his wife, Sandra, joined her in Santa Fe to begin the asylum application process. Cipriana's case, to their surprise, moved quickly: after filing the application in January 2011, Cipriana was granted her first interview in March. Her application was approved in June.

Despite this success, however, life in the United States has not been easy for Cipriana or her children: her son struggled with serious depression and Cipriana with feelings of guilt for her inability to help her community back in Mexico. "Then on top of that, here you have to start over from zero," she says. With limited English, Cipriana has fewer employment options and has had to do a little bit of everything: cleaning houses, babysitting, cooking, selling jewelry, transcribing interviews. Adjusting to the U.S. financial system has been a challenge as well: "In Mexico, the fewer debts you have, the better, but here if you have debts and pay them off on time, that's good for your credit. No one tells you that; you have to figure it out as you go . . . In Mexico, if you rent, and you fall behind a month, you can negotiate with the landlords. Here, no, you have to pay the bills no matter what. Here, everything's controlled by companies, big and small, not people with faces. There's no humanity, they just charge interest."

In addition to taking English classes at a local community college, Cipriana has been one of the mainstays of a nonprofit organization called Mexicanos en Exilio (Mexicans in Exile), which developed out of Carlos Spector's work over the past few years. The organization, known as MexenEx in El Paso, channels the efforts of Carlos and his team to provide free legal advice to those seeking asylum and to help them start their new lives in the United States. Cipriana is the president of the board of directors; Martha Valles, sister of Marisol Valles, the former chief of police in Práxedis, Guerrero, also sits on the board, as does Saúl Reyes, a cofounder of the organization. "Our primary goal is justice," Cipriana says; asylum, while important, is secondary.

"I knew the organization was feasible in 2008, but I started looking around for leaders, because I knew the group would not grow unless it was led by members of the affected community," Carlos explains. "I knew the character of the group would be defined by them." He continues to play a prominent role in the organization's public events, however, because he crafts the legal strategy that then influences the group's political work. When the Alvarado girls were looking for information on their mother, for instance, the group organized a protest in front of the Mexican Consulate. "That way we're killing two birds with one stone," Carlos explains.

"We're sending a message, and making progress on one of the cases. That is the group's success. Every time we make progress on one family's case, we're making progress for everyone's case."

Part of MexenEx's political strategy is to publicize the cases of murdered activists. One such activist is Marisela Escobedo, killed in the city of Chihuahua in 2010 in front of the Government Palace, while she was protesting the murder of her daughter, Ruby Marisol Frayre, in Juárez two years earlier. The Escobedo family had investigated the killing, to which Héctor Escobedo, Marisela's brother, had been an eyewitness. MexenEx succeeded in pressuring the Mexican government into taking an official declaration from Marisela's son Juan Frayre, who maintained all along that he knew who had murdered his mother: the brother of Ruby Marisol's confessed killer. In 2015, Carlos won political asylum for Juan.

Another MexenEx case that made headlines was that of Carlos Gutiérrez, a businessman from the city of Chihuahua, whom I met in Carlos Spector's office in 2012, and who had once led a relatively stable life in Mexico with his wife and two children. In 2011, he was extorted by armed criminal groups, who demanded that he pay them $10,000 for the right to continue operating his business. Calling the police would have been useless, he says, so he agreed to pay the extortionists. But as violence escalated throughout the state, business declined, and eventually he could not make the payment. The extortionists kidnapped him, took him to a remote spot, and sawed off his feet as a warning to other businessmen, leaving him for dead.

After miraculously surviving the attack, Carlos made his way to El Paso, where his legs had to be amputated below the knee. Disabled, traumatized, with no money, he contacted Carlos Spector and began the process of applying for political asylum. The case stalled, leaving Carlos Gutiérrez in legal limbo, allowed to stay in the United States but without access to citizenship.

A doctor in El Paso fitted Carlos with prosthetic limbs at no cost. To recover from the surgery, he began riding a bicycle. Two years later, with the support of MexenEx, he rode seven hundred miles in twelve days from El Paso to Austin. He wore shorts, his prosthetic legs in full view, to raise awareness of the plight of Mexicans who seek political asylum.

As we talk about these cases, Carlos Spector grows indignant. As these Mexicans fight for their rights here and start their lives over again, he says, those back in Mexico are largely forgotten. Many U.S. judges, Cipriana points out, don't understand that although Enrique Peña Nieto has taken over from Felipe Calderón, "and that even though some narco bosses and military officers have been arrested, that doesn't mean things have changed locally, or that people who left can go back now." Paying an extortionist or a kidnapper is illegal in the United States; in Mexico, it is often the only option.

MexenEx's greatest achievement, Carlos says, has been to create a model of cooperation between citizens in the two countries. "Here in the United States we're ready and willing, with resources and with exiled Mexicans who are still angry, and want to do something," he notes. "But we can't do it alone, and Mexico can't either—we need each other."

Furthermore, Carlos says, the organization's success depends on Mexicans' willingness to share their stories about the incredible violence in Mexico, about which most

Americans are ignorant. "The only way to let people know," he says, "is for these Mexicans to talk about it themselves." The organization's work is further complicated by the fact that its membership is always in flux, as Cipriana points out. "Once some people get their legal status straightened out," she notes, "they don't feel the need to keep on working with the organization." Many are forced to leave El Paso to look for work; others leave "for security reasons."

MexenEx, Carlos says, is part of the "New Juárez" in El Paso, where the approximately 100,000 exiles from violence in Chihuahua during the Calderón administration, most of them from Juárez, have moved. "There are many categories of people who make up this new exile community," he explains, including people with dual citizenship, permanent residency, and visas who have entered the country legally. "Now, the time has come to activate this community."

In addition to his work with MexenEx, Carlos hopes to change how the law is applied in relation to organized crime. Asylum petitions must be based on one of five categories, one of which is political opinion; resisting extortion, Carlos argues, should qualify as the basis for an asylum petition because it is a political act.

"If the state is managing the extortion, if the state itself is organized crime, and you decide not to accept being extorted, and you don't pay, you are performing an act of civil resistance, a political act. Internationally, and in U.S. jurisprudence, it is acknowledged that when the state extorts you, a political act has taken place. If the state controls crime, then the crime is happening with the support of the state. The major political challenge is to change the terms of the debate and debunk this myth of organized crime . . . Out of the one hundred cases of asylum I have, I can show you that in every case of repression or persecution, the state is directly or indirectly involved . . .

"For me, this movement starts with Mexican communities here and there who make demands on systems and institutions . . . That's where we have to start, to create a culture of insisting and forcing the government to respond to people's concerns . . . We don't have financial or political resources on a national level, but we do have our voices."

# 12

# The Never-Ending Wave

Rosario is slender, with a dark complexion, long black hair, and an easy smile. Wearing skinny jeans, sneakers, and a T-shirt, she sits in a waiting room between two men dressed in suits, busily sending text messages on their phones. Any minute now, she will be called in to one of the rooms in this building of long, white hallways and cool walls that houses Federal Immigration Court. Just fourteen years old, with no lawyer to represent her, Rosario is about to sit before a judge for the first time in her young life.

Rosario and her brother José, fifteen, arrived in the United States a few months earlier from Sensuntepeque, El Salvador. They belong to a statistic that alarmed authorities and the general public in the summer of 2014: in the first nine months of the fiscal year beginning in October 2014, over 52,000 minors under the age of eighteen were detained along the Mexican border while trying to enter the country undocumented and unaccompanied by an adult. During the same period of the previous year, according to the Department of

Homeland Security, 26,000 young people were detained. Three out of four were over the age of fourteen. These adolescents were leaving Honduras, El Salvador, Guatemala, and Mexico to be reunited with their parents in the United States, to find work, and to escape violence.

A report from the United Nations High Commissioner for Refugees (UNHCR) published at the time found in interviews of hundreds of these young people that at least 58 percent had been "forcibly displaced because they faced harms that indicated a potential or actual need for international protection." Half said they had been affected by a rise in violence in their communities perpetrated by organized crime, gangs, or the state itself. Twenty-two percent said they had been victims of physical abuse in their own homes, at the hands of the adult responsible for caring for them. Eleven percent said they had been victimized both in their own homes and in their communities. Thirty-eight percent of the children coming from Mexico said they had been the victims or potential victims of recruitment or exploitation by criminal gangs.

These young people were candidates for political asylum or for humanitarian visas, according to international agreements and current U.S. asylum laws. But the U.S. government is not obligated to provide them with free legal counsel; therefore they must go before an immigration court judge without a lawyer representing them. It is up to the judge to explain to them their options for staying in the country.

María is Rosario and José's mother. She is thirty-three years old, and left her country, El Salvador, seven years ago, leaving her five children in her mother's care. Since arriving in the United States, she has worked in the fields in California, planting and picking. She does not speak English and can barely read or write. Still, she found a way to save money and send some to El Salvador. When she had saved up $18,000, the fee a "trustworthy" coyote would charge for bringing over her two eldest children, she did not hesitate.

"They told me it was so expensive because it was safe, and they wouldn't suffer," María told me, as we stood in a hallway in the courthouse. A short woman—her two children are already taller than her—her anguish shows on her face as she talks about the threats her family experienced. One night some men came to her mother's house to demand an extortion payment. María's mother handed over the money she had, but the men still threatened to return for more. That was when María decided to send for her children.

"They promised me they would be comfortable, in a car, they would get here no problem," she tells me. "But it wasn't like that. They made them walk, and ride on the luggage rack of a bus, and in the end, look what happened, they were caught."

The migration of unaccompanied minors did not suddenly begin with the "surge" in 2014. This kind of migration was first reported in detail in 2002 by journalist Sonia Nazario, in a series of articles in the *Los Angeles Times*. Nazario wrote about Enrique, a boy traveling alone from Honduras to join his mother in the United States. The series included photos of Enrique riding on top of the freight train known as "The Beast," which became iconic images of Central American migration. In 2006 Nazario won a Pulitzer Prize for the series; she adapted it into a book titled *Enrique's Journey*, which became a best seller and was published in eight languages.

In the last decade, hundreds of articles and books have been published about migration by adults and minors through Mexico featuring harrowing images of migrants riding on "The Beast," even though only 18 percent of migrants traveling through Mexico take the train. Over that time, the demographics of the travelers have changed: between 2012 and 2014, the overall number of unaccompanied minors grew and the percentage of girls rose from 23 to 27 percent. The number of children younger than fourteen years old grew from 17 to 24 percent.

When Rosario and José were detained by the authorities, María got a call. She was told that her children were being held in the immigration detention center in Los Angeles, and that she had to begin the process to have them released. According to the law, minors cannot remain in the custody of immigration authorities for more than seventy-two hours, after which they are transferred to temporary shelters run by the Office of Refugee Resettlement (ORR). On average, eight out of every ten unaccompanied minors will spend some time in one of these shelters. Some areas, especially in South Texas, were struggling to meet the seventy-two-hour requirement at the time, due to the government's inability to process all of the minors coming in.

After a few days, María's children were transferred to a shelter, where they would remain until their mother could prove her identity and demonstrate that she could financially support them. María lived in a garage that had been converted into a living space. But in order to have her children live with her, the law required that she live in a home with at least one bedroom. María had to work overtime to save up enough money to put down a deposit on an apartment that met that requirement, so she could have her children released to her.

Once María was reunited with her children, they received a notice that a process of deportation had been started, along with an order to appear before an immigration judge. With little money, no English, and no understanding of the U.S. legal system, María did not know what to do to ensure that her children would not be returned to El Salvador. All she knew was that they had to appear in court on the day and at the time indicated by the notice.

When an official calls out her children's names, María and her children go into the courtroom and sit down on a bench before a judge. On the wall behind her hangs an enormous seal of the United States Department of Justice. There is an interpreter with the judge. María and her children put on headphones to hear the proceedings in Spanish. Her eyes wide, María hesitates before answering the judge's questions. At one point, she says she does not understand what is being said. The judge explains that the person sitting next to them is an attorney representing the U.S. government, which has accused them of being in the country without documentation. The judge asks if they have a lawyer. Rosario's leg shakes nervously. José does not say a word.

In discussions of the Central American exiles fleeing to the United States, one key factor in the equation is often omitted: that the violence in the region directly stems from its relationship with the United States. The U.S. military and Central Intelligence Agency supported and trained repressive military forces in Central America. Weapons from U.S. manufacturers wind up in the hands of criminal groups,

many of which have ties to the government. Illicit drugs traf-
ficked through Central America easily find consumers in the
large U.S. market for them. The United States deports young
gang members from its cities who harass and terrorize other
young people back in their home countries. Their victims
are forced to flee to the United States, where they are denied
asylum. And the cycle repeats.

While peace treaties signed in Central America—in
Nicaragua in 1990, El Salvador in 1992, and Guatemala in
1996—were designed to improve conditions in the region,
active and retired military personnel have since created their
own centers of power outside of the government, fomenting
organized crime. Military dependence on the United States
gave way to economic dependence on foreign corporations
and an unstable labor market.

The illegal arms trade, including weapons from army
arsenals which wind up in criminal hands, only exacerbates
the situation. This illicit market was also "Made in the USA":
at gun shows along the border with Mexico, AK-47 assault
rifles, also known as "cuernos de chivo" (goat horns), and
other high-powered weapons are easy to find and purchase
legally, after which they are transported by car southward,
over the border.[1]

It is estimated that approximately 2,000 weapons enter
Mexico from the United States every day, many of which can
then be traced to Guatemala. The Tepito crime cartel, headquartered in Mexico City, has at least thirty-five points of
sale of weapons transported from the United States or stolen
from Mexico's secretary of national defense. Forty percent
of the traced weapons introduced illegally in Mexico come
from Houston, Dallas, and McAllen, Texas.[2]

In public discourse, the "maras" (gangs) are portrayed as the main threat to public safety in the region, criminalizing young men and reinforcing stereotypes. These gangs absorbed the gangs that had already been operating in Guatemala, Honduras, and El Salvador, in what is called a "glocal" phenomenon: groups that comprise a network of gangs with transnational connections but operate with local autonomy. This phenomenon was fueled by massive deportations of gang members with criminal charges from the United States.

Along with a rise in criminal gangs, large-scale migration from El Salvador to the United States surged in the 1990s even as peace treaties were being signed—although, like Mexico, El Salvador already had a long history of migration going back at least as far as the nineteenth century. Just as with most immigrants who arrive in the United States undocumented and from impoverished regions, young migrants from Central America settled in cities and towns across the country with Central American communities. Searching for a sense of belonging, some joined gangs whose members tended to be from immigrant families. Although gangs are active all over the country, they are most prevalent in New York, where the first gangs were made up of European immigrants in the late nineteenth century; Chicago, which had a dramatic surge in organized crime activity in the 1930s; and, most recently, Los Angeles.[3]

Los Angeles has a large population of Salvadoran migrants and a long history of gangs, two of which have attracted particular notice recently: Mara Salvatrucha (MS-13 or MS) and Barrio 18. The former was started by Salvadoran men and women in Los Angeles who had fled the civil war and political violence in their country in the 1980s. They have a nationalist bent and incorporate symbols of Salvadoran culture into their style, in the Chicano fashion. Many members of Barrio 18 come from Mexico and other Central American countries.

After immigration policies hardened in the wake of the terrorist attacks of September 11, 2001, these gangs were seen as a threat to national security. As we have already seen, one consequence of stricter immigration measures has been an exponential increase in rates of detentions and deportations, compared with rates in the 1990s. In 1993, 2,117 Salvadorans were deported; ten years later, in 2003, that figure rose to 5,561, and in 2009, to over 20,000. In 2016, over 52,000 Salvadorans were deported.

"If the right to asylum were based on some kind of moral responsibility within a historical context," argues Mario Zúñiga, associate professor of anthropology at the University of Costa Rica and an expert in Central American migration, then the United States would be obligated to act as "an almost exclusive refuge." Humanitarian organizations, he points out, have ignored U.S. culpability in the refugee crisis, and instead "have separated out asylum petitions from the historical context, and focused on the children, the segment of the population that can most effectively inspire compassion in the general public."[4] At the height of the migration of unaccompanied minors, in 2014, children represented only one quarter of the total number of migrants arriving from Central America. Adults flee their countries due to the same cycles of violence that children are escaping.

"The problem is migration became something political," Erick Midence says in a tone between reproachful and ironic.

"The children are detained, they're put into deportation proceedings because that's the law, but they're not deported . . . because that would have a political cost, and neither the president [nor] the Republicans want to pay it. They can say what they want, but in practice, the kids stay here."

An activist for almost two decades and president of the Honduran Association of Oxnard, a small city north of Los Angeles, Erick found out about María's case and offered to go to court with her. He is not a lawyer, but over the years he has learned how to handle deportation proceedings. In theory, Rosario and José have to go to court to listen to the charges of being in the country illegally. If they accept the charges, the judge issues an order of deportation and they are returned to El Salvador. If they do not accept the charges, they must present supporting evidence. The goal, however, is to try to buy more time in order to stay in the country for a few more years, even though they still may not win legal status. They can ask for up to two extensions. They then can appeal an unfavorable ruling, which will buy them more time. The judges know about this strategy but continue to grant extensions. Children who entered the country undocumented are still here two, three, four years later.

Statistics from the Department of Homeland Security confirm this. In the fiscal years 2012 through 2015, over 171,000 minors under the age of eighteen were detained, but only 7,643 minors were deported.[5] Those deported either signed an agreement to leave the country voluntarily or lost their cases in immigration court and decided not to appeal.

The deportation process has become a sort of prolonged grace period because of the enormous backlog of cases pending in immigration courts. It could take two or three years to receive a final judgment in a case, with extensions, and then around three years more if an appeal is filed. During this time, the young people remain in the United States with family members. If they are fleeing danger in their home countries, that is a victory in itself. But many children are stuck in legal limbo without a qualified lawyer to ensure that they arrive in court with substantiating evidence that would allow them to legalize their status. Not surprisingly, these children and their families can be easy prey for unscrupulous lawyers who offer to evaluate their cases for huge fees, only to tell them later that there is nothing to be done.

The judge gives Maria and her children a date in six months to appear in court, with a lawyer.

It's 9:20 in the morning when Mario Saavedra walks into the office building at 3550 Wilshire Boulevard, Los Angeles. Wearing dress pants and a crisp shirt, both neatly ironed, and newly shined black shoes, he goes up to the third floor and walks down the hallway until he finds a door displaying the national shield of Honduras. He has an appointment to speak with a functionary at the consulate at 9:30.

An hour passes, and he has still not been seen by anyone. Mario tries to be patient, but he is growing desperate. Two weeks ago he got a call from U.S. immigration authorities. They told him that his daughter Fernanda, fourteen, had been detained while crossing the Texas border into the United States, undocumented. He was not given a number that he could call, or told where his daughter was.

A few days later, his daughter called him. She was in a shelter, but she did not know where. She sobbed until the call was cut off. Calls from shelters are limited to three minutes, and the number is blocked. Mario was left staring at the phone in his hand, not knowing what to do.

Fernanda is one of the 52,000 minors detained in 2014 and managed by an improvised system thrown together to address the large number of cases that year. It's June 2014, and President Barack Obama has just declared the migrant crisis a state of emergency, calling for an inter-agency response involving immigration authorities, the Federal Emergency Management Administration (FEMA), and the Department of Justice. The government opened three shelters for 120 days at military bases in California, Oklahoma, and Texas, which housed 3,000 unaccompanied minors. The president also requested a budget of $1.5 billion in emergency funds to pay for the minors' shelter, food, and transportation, on top of the $868 million already appropriated by Congress for fiscal year 2014. The expensive process of identifying and evaluating each minor, contacting their families, and verifying that the family member is qualified to receive them can take weeks. For parents waiting to be reunited with their children, this bureaucratic process is a nightmare.

Mario lives in Bakersfield, two hours north of Los Angeles. This city has been his home for eleven years, since he arrived from Sonaguera, Honduras. He has worked in the fields and construction and currently installs wood floors.

Mario was twenty-five when he and his wife left Honduras in 2003. His mother remained in Honduras with his daughter Fernanda, who was three years old at the time. After arriving in the United States, Mario and his wife separated, but he continued providing his daughter with financial and emotional support.

"I had no idea she was going to come here," he says, anguished, as he waits in the consulate. He clutches a large manila envelope stuffed with documents. During their weekly phone calls, his daughter had never mentioned what she was planning to do. "How could I let her do that when I know how dangerous it is?" he says. "But my mother is seventy years old, and my daughter didn't listen to her anymore."

An hour and a half later, Interim Consul José María Tsai meets with Mario. Tsai has been in charge of the consul for five months, and he is unsure what to do. Sitting in front of a giant Honduran flag, with a neutral expression, he explains to Mario that the Department of Homeland Security has opened a hotline just for parents. If he calls the number, they will give him information, take his phone number, and try to get him in touch with his daughter. There is nothing more Tsai can do.

As soon as young people are transferred to the shelters, members of civil organizations that support migrants assess their health and try to provide legal assistance. This stage is crucial for the child's future. It is common for the minors to lie to the social workers or lawyers interviewing them at the shelters. The "coyotes" who were hired to guide them north often coach them to give false answers. Only after several days are the interviewers able to break the ice and identify signs of abuse, or indications that the child has been threatened by criminal gangs or abandoned. With proper legal representation, these children might gain legal status to stay in the United States through an application for asylum or a humanitarian visa.

At the same time, a social worker tries to make contact with a family member in the United States. Since most of these children travel with false documents or with no documents at all, their identities need to be confirmed; then the closest family member needs to be identified as the child's sponsor. This can be a delicate process. Many of the children are reunited with family members they have not seen in years. Joyce Capelle, president of Crittenton, a shelter in Southern California, tells me that some children have asked not to be sent away with fathers who have physically abused them. In that case, the shelter interrupts the process to perform detailed interviews with often far-flung relatives. "The last thing we want is to release the child to someone who could be a trafficker or will abuse him," Capelle explains.

According to the Department of Homeland Security, unaccompanied minors spend thirty-five days on average in these temporary shelters. But some children spend months in places like Crittenton before it is deemed safe to release them. The problem is that while the number of unaccompanied minors crossing the border has increased, resources for managing them have begun to diminish. In 2014 and 2015, many organizations serving migrants began soliciting donations online in order to continue doing their work.

As soon as he left the Honduran Consulate, Mario called the DHS hotline for parents. He was told that Fernanda had been transferred from Texas to a shelter on a military base in Oklahoma. After demonstrating that he was Fernanda's father and that he was financially able to support her, he was told he would be reunited with his daughter within a week. Then, he and Fernanda would receive a notice to appear in immigration court. With good legal representation, they may be able to prove that Fernanda was fleeing a life-threatening situation and apply for asylum or a humanitarian visa. Legal maneuvers may buy them a few years of time so Fernanda can stay in the country. And perhaps something better will come along: immigration or legal reform that will mean they won't have to be separated again.

# 13

## *"We don't want you here!"*

"We don't want you! Go home!" A man's enraged scream rises above the crowd brandishing signs around three white buses. The buses, blazoned with the Department of Homeland Security (DHS) logo, are transporting 140 undocumented immigrants, mostly children and adolescents. The immigrants were detained in Texas; now they are being transferred for processing at facilities run by immigration authorities in Murrieta, California. They never make it.

The crowd of around 200 people brandishing signs with anti-immigrant slogans block the buses, forcing them to change their route and head toward San Diego. The protesters celebrate this victory in an ongoing effort to make sure that the over 50,000 children who have arrived in the United States that year will be returned to their home countries. These demonstrators do not understand that if their efforts succeed, the lives of most of these children will be in danger.

The interviews in the 2014 report by the United Nations High Commissioner on Refugees (UNHCR) clearly demonstrate this dark reality. Migrant children have suffered extreme poverty and violence at the hands of armed criminals, the state, and their caretakers. The report concluded that the governments of their countries of origin cannot safeguard the most basic rights of these individuals, and that the international community must therefore protect them. People fleeing from armed conflicts, serious internal disorder, massive human rights violations, generalized violence, and other forms of serious harm should be considered as candidates for legal protection.

It is no coincidence that these children head to the United States. Although geographic proximity and family ties help determine the route of exodus, UNHCR data shows that in 2012, the United States, which has some of the most demanding asylum laws on the planet, nevertheless received over 85 percent of all asylum applications filed around the world.

A row of American flags, motionless under the hundred-degree July sun, welcomes visitors to Murrieta, where the stifling afternoon passes slowly. Time also seems to have come to a standstill on some of the street corners, where the antique shop, post office, small general stores, and repair shops conjure up a quintessential town of the Old West. A car pulls to a stop at an intersection, and its driver, a man with a long mustache, dark sunglasses, and a hat, gives me a perfunctory glance before going on his way.

Murrieta is a typical small American city. Located in Southern California's semi-desert Inland Empire region, Murrieta and its neighboring city, Temecula, lie in a valley where the arid landscape on the outskirts of the Sonora desert gives way to a green patch dotted with large shopping centers of red and orange bricks. Two major highways, Interstates 15 and 215, run alongside the city's avenues, which are named after the founding fathers: Washington, Jefferson, Adams, Monroe. Seven of every ten residents are white, and one in four are Latino. Murrieta's official motto is "the future of Southern California."

Murrieta rarely made the nightly news or appeared in the headlines before July 1, 2014, when an angry crowd gathered along the side of the road to wait for three ICE vehicles carrying migrant children detained at the border. Shouting slogans against illegal immigration, holding up signs accusing the children of carrying contagious diseases, and with occasional outbursts of uncontrollable anger and vitriol, a few dozen local residents stood across the road to block the path of the buses and force the immigration convoy to turn around. *"We don't want you, go home!"* a woman overcome with hatred screamed, right in front of the face of a stunned boy inside one of the buses, peering through the window, his eyes open wide, before the buses drove away.

"What the federal government is doing is wrong; it's inhumane," says Diana Serafin, one of the organizers of the Murrieta protest. "You can't ship people from one place to another like they're animals, not knowing if they're diseased, without treating them, without making sure they're okay after they crossed the border." She hurls this accusation indignantly, her use of "ship" suggesting the movement of inanimate merchandise. Sixty-three years old and slender, with chestnut hair framing a face with small eyes and a broad smile, she talks with the energy of an impassioned twenty-something. The day we meet, a month after the incident with the buses, she is wearing a T-shirt emblazoned with the American flag.

Diana got the word out about the arrival of the migrant children through her Twitter account, where she describes herself as "a Patriot defending Freedom, Liberty and the Constitution." The information she distributed warned that the children carried scabies, tuberculosis and the ebola virus and that Islamic terrorists enter the United States through its southern border.

"This isn't about attacking immigrants," Diana says. "It's about protecting children. Our issue is about the conditions they were brought here under." The Border Patrol facilities, she says, are like prisons: "cement beds, metal bars, a cell with a toilet right there. They were going to make them eat right next to the toilet! . . . The federal government is using these children politically, they don't care about their well-being." Without a family member to come get them, Diana says, the children would be dropped off at the nearest bus stop to fend for themselves.

"Can you imagine what a teenager could do, desperate, not speaking English, with no money, not knowing the country?" Diana says vehemently. "Desperation can lead to terrible things. How could the government create a situation like that?"

Diana's Twitter bio links to her personal website, where she announces her intention to run for a seat on the Murrieta City Council and includes a list of people supporting her candidacy. These include California State Assemblyman Tim Donnelly, who founded California's Minuteman Party; the goal of the Minuteman movement is to guard the border in order to ensure that no immigrants cross over illegally. In

2010, he courted the Tea Party vote to win the Republican party nomination and a seat in the state assembly.

Diana identifies with Donnelly's agenda and that of Alan Long, the young, conservative mayor of Murrieta. Long openly opposed the federal government's decision to send migrant children to Murrieta, calling on city residents at a press conference on June 30 to contact their representatives in Congress and tell them to stop the children from coming. The violent roadside protest took place the following day. And on July 2, over 1,500 local residents attended a community meeting. Long sent a letter to President Obama on July 3, assuring him that Long's administration had not provoked the events that had occurred between his press conference and the community meeting.

Maria Carrillo, originally from Mexico, has lived in the United States since she was three years old and in Murrieta and Temecula for thirteen years. She asserts that Long uses the issue of migration for his own political purposes. We meet at a Starbucks a few blocks from where I spoke with Diana. She tells me that in all her years in Murrieta, she had never experienced a racist incident. Then, a few days before the roadside protest, her eighteen-year-old daughter, Carissa, encountered a confrontation between pro- and anti-immigrant activists at a Walmart. "She was really surprised by the level of verbal violence," Maria says. "When one of the protesters saw that she was Latina, he started yelling at her. He told her to get the hell out of there, and told her to go wash his car."

When Maria attended the community meeting on July 2, which she thought would be focused on "doing something for the children," her feelings of being in the minority intensified. The mayor, she says, "congratulated everyone there for what they had done the day before, for defending the city." Attendees emphasized that the children were carrying diseases. And of all the attendees, "only three or four or us were Latinos," she says. Since the meeting, her feelings of vulnerability have increased. "I know there are a lot of people who sympathize with the children, but they don't say it in public because they don't want to get attacked."

William Young found out about the actions to "support the Border Patrol" and keep the children from arriving through Diana Serafin's Twitter campaign. Young is around sixty years old and married with two children. A Cardinals fan who served in the U.S. Marines for twenty-four years, he describes himself as a "conservative Christian," not affiliated with any organization but sympathetic to the views of those demonstrating against the migrants' arrival. "I'm not racist," he maintains. "How could I be, since I'm African American?"

William is upset with the media's portrayals of the road-side protest. He maintains that the most aggressive acts were committed by outsiders, not residents of Murrieta. Those outsiders received the most media attention, William says, because they were the most scandalous—including the demonstrator who spat in the face of Lupillo Rivera, a popular singer of the genre known as "regional Mexican," who was there to welcome the migrant children.

The children and women who cross the border, William says, are "being exploited on several levels. They're used by their own governments, by narcotrafficking cartels, by the coyotes, and our government." The immigrants arriving without documentation have other ways of entering the country, he and Diana argue, as do many others who oppose the arrival of the migrant children. But they would rather take "the fast track." "These people have come looking for options in the United States instead of staying in their countries and fighting for their governments to improve the situation," William says. "If they come here, they should do it the right way."

Then I ask William if he is aware that citizens of countries including El Salvador, Guatemala, and Mexico cannot enter the visa lottery. If they are not sponsored by an employer, or if a family member does not petition for them, these people have no other way to come to the United States legally.

"Is that true?" William asks, genuinely surprised. "You mean they can't go to the consulate and apply for a visa to come here and work?"

The former marine mulls it over, then takes up his position again.

"See? That's what I'm talking about. Obama's making this happen. They should talk to the governments of those countries to change the law. My issue is not with the people, I'm mad at a government that's not doing its job."

At the end of our conversation, William asks me one last question.

"And since you seem to know about this, tell me, if they're leaving Guatemala or El Salvador, why do they come to the United States? Why don't they stay in Mexico? Why doesn't Mexico do anything to help them?"

Murrieta is an hour away from San Diego, the home of Border Angels director Enrique Morones. The area is also home to a small but entrenched network of activist organizations working against illegal immigration. I had been in sporadic contact with Enrique ever since we traveled together in the Migrant Caravan along the Mexican border in 2007. When the issue of child migrants intensified, our conversations resumed.

Enrique has two telephone numbers. One number, which he never answers, gets voicemails from anti-immigrant groups who constantly threaten and harass him. At first these calls disturbed him, but he has learned to live with it. His other number, a private one, gets calls from people seeking his organization's help. The last time I saw him, he got a call from someone asking if he could help transport two children, ages four and nine, who had entered the country unaccompanied and were going to be reunited with their mother.

Although his day-to-day contact with anti-immigrant groups is usually limited to voicemails, Enrique came face to face with them in Murrieta during the roadside protest. "It's our obligation as a country" to receive these children, Enrique argues, "but Americans don't want to hear it."

The Convention of the Rights of the Child maintains that the best interests of a child must be a primary consideration in all administrative and legal proceedings. But a report titled "A Treacherous Journey: Child Migrants Navigating the U.S. Immigration System" from the Center for Gender and Refugee Studies at the University of California Hastings, in cooperation with the organization Kids in Need of Defense, found that the U.S. government does not use this standard in its treatment of migrant children, rarely providing assistance or counseling to minors who have been victims of human trafficking and other abuses. The report states that "some immigration judges have rejected social groups in children's cases based on size, fearing that approving broadly defined groups will open the proverbial floodgates while not recognizing that establishing social group membership fulfills only one element of an asylum claim." Immigration courts have refused to recognize as vulnerable social groups some of the most exposed who ask for protection, including "girls who report their rape to the police," "youth who oppose gang activity and have reported it to the police," and "young girls who resisted gang recruitment and witnessed gang crime," among others.

The treacherous journey across Mexico, inclement weather, abuse from government agents and extortionists, and fear of leaving her home were just some of challenges Ileana faced when she set off from her country in Central America to try to enter the United States undocumented.[1] But none of that compared, according to the fifteen-year-old, to the eleven days she spent locked up by U.S. immigration, abused, unprotected, and denied access to basic services.

Since the surge in unaccompanied minors began, and in spite of the (clearly inadequate) efforts of immigration authorities, charges of abuse filed against the Border Patrol and other security agencies, including treatment that could be considered torture, have risen sharply. Groups of lawyers and activists have increased pressure on the government to take legal action, such as suspending the deportation of some of these youth who qualify for a U visa, granted to those who "have suffered substantial mental or physical abuse as a result of having been the victim of criminal activity" that "occurred in the United States or violated U.S. laws."[2]

Ileana's case, handled by the New York law firm Amoachi & Johnson, serves as a good example of this. When Ileana was detained by Border Patrol agents in Texas, according to her lawsuit, the first violation of her rights she experienced was overcrowding. She was locked in a confined space with over a hundred other people, including women, small children, and other teens, and not even enough room to lie down, she told her lawyers weeks later. In the days that followed, she experienced a series of rights violations: lack of food or food that had spoiled, lack of safe drinking water, freezing temperatures, and housing conditions violating standards in U.S. legislation. Once she had been released from the detention center, she cataloged these violations and others as she was filing her suit. Ileana's lawyers presented a request to the Justice Department to have her deportation order annulled, given that the immigration authorities had interviewed her regarding her eligibility for asylum under conditions of detainment that violated all rules.

As one of her lawyers, Bryan Johnson, recounted to me, Ileana was in the border processing center for four days (rather than the mandated seventy-two hours), then transferred to a military shelter in Oklahoma for seven days, during which time she lost eight pounds. "She ate practically nothing during that time," Bryan says. "She was kept in very cold temperatures, with fluorescent lights turned on all day and all night"—conditions experienced by "almost every kid who entered the country between July and August," he points out.

These statements, researched and verified by his legal team, are corroborated by accounts published in the media and from activist organizations: H., a seven-year-old boy with a disability and severely malnourished at the time of his detention, was detained in Customs and Border Patrol

(CBP) custody for five days without access to medical treatment. When he was finally released, he had to undergo emergency surgery. D., a sixteen-year-old girl, was held in a detention cell with adults. When agents searched her, they violently spread her legs and touched her genitals. K., a fourteen-year-old girl with asthma, had her medicine confiscated when she was detained by CBP agents. During her time in the overcrowded cell, she suffered several asthma attacks. Guards threatened to discipline her if she kept on "faking it." C., a seventeen-year-old girl, was held in a freezing cell—what detainees call the "hielera" ("freezer")—wearing wet clothes. It took three days for her clothes to dry. The only potable water was in the toilet tank, in full view of the other detainees, with a video camera over it.

In June 2014, these testimonies were included in a legal complaint presented to Department of Homeland Security (DHS) authorities by a coalition of activist and human rights organizations, including the American Civil Liberties Union (ACLU) and the National Immigrant Justice Center (NIJC). The document included testimony from 116 children between the ages of six and seventeen, who were interviewed at the temporary shelters run by the Department of Health and Human Services about the mistreatment they'd experienced in DHS custody.

Jonathan Ryan is the executive director of the Refugee and Immigrant Center for Education and Legal Services (RAICES), an organization headquartered in Texas. During the summer of 2014, the organization received more calls asking for help than ever before, describing the horrible conditions and abuse children had suffered in custody. The surge in migrant children traveling alone "tested the government's capacity much more than any of them would admit," Jonathan tells me a few months later on the phone. A lawyer by profession, he and I first met at a forum on immigration in San Antonio. While acknowledging that some of the installations may have been overcrowded, Jonathan asserts that some of the inhumane practices denounced that summer are nothing unusual in immigrant detention.

"This wasn't because of a lack of resources," he says. "For example, temperatures in cells where the children were held were kept at an average of 55 degrees Fahrenheit. Maintaining this temperature in South Texas, in the height of summer, implies an allocation of resources in an additional effort to make them uncomfortable, to disincentivize them and discourage them from continuing to seek asylum."

While in the processing center, immigration agents interviewed the unaccompanied minors to determine if they were eligible to seek political asylum or some other form of humanitarian relief. But the majority of these children, like Ileana, were interviewed under prison-like conditions, which likely produced a disheartening effect. Under this pressure, many of them signed a form authorizing their voluntary removal from the country. In our conversation, Jonathan confirms the pattern of abuse of unaccompanied minors in immigrant processing facilities, the same one described by Ileana's attorneys and the coalition of organizations who filed the complaint in June 2014.

"It's not just the physical conditions," Jonathan says. "It's the psychological abuse too. The kids describe harsh language, and a lack of respect. They are told they don't have any right to be there, or to apply for asylum." The officials' priority, he says, rather than ensuring the children's welfare, is "making them leave the country as soon as possible."

When the attorneys of Amoachi & Johnson made their complaint public on December 11, 2014, they elevated the tone of the discussion in two ways. First, they sent their request to annul Ileana's deportation not to the Department of Homeland Security, but to the Department of Justice (DOJ), asking the DOJ to review the treatment of unaccompanied minors by Customs and Border Patrol. Second, the lawyers explicitly categorized Ileana's treatment as torture.

In their public briefing, the firm cited documents published that year by the Obama administration regarding torture implemented by the Central Intelligence Agency (CIA). They pointed out that the DHS had created conditions for detaining migrant children "identical to what the CIA used to detain suspected terrorists during the Bush administration"—conditions that had been condemned by President Obama as having "significantly damaged the image of the United States throughout the world," the lawyers explained. Over ten pages, they detailed the treatment Ileana had received, including being deprived of food, water, clothing, and blankets and forbidden to bathe or change clothes. Ileana, they wrote, "saw other children ask for the air conditioning to be turned off; CBP agents denied their requests and told the children they were nothing more than 'abandoned dogs.'" By recording the verbal abuse and psychological abuse of these children, the lawyers hope to improve their conditions and stop their deportation proceedings. A preliminary response from the DHS Inspector General

ordered an investigation into the conditions at some processing centers. To the lawyers, the issue goes beyond that: they
see the necessity of tallying verbal and psychological abuse,
and ensuring that considerations are put in place for these
children, including stopping their deportation proceedings.
Those who break the law saying "we don't want you here"
may become the reason they stay here.

# Epilogue

On April 6, 2017, at 7:40 p.m. Eastern Standard Time, President Donald Trump ordered an attack on Syria. Fifty-nine Tomahawk missiles were launched on an air base, killing over eighty civilians. The attack was carried out sixty-three hours after the Syrian government used chemical weapons against civilians in a rebel-controlled province, killing hundreds of women and children who were suffocated by the effects of sarin gas, which damages the nervous system. A few hours after that attack, Trump justified his actions in advance. "When you kill innocent children, innocent babies, little babies, with a chemical gas that was so lethal," he announced, "that crosses many lines, beyond a red line, many many lines."

Trump's response to the killing of children, however, did not include revising his position on asylum law, nor did it entail any initiative to welcome refugees from Syrian president Bashar al-Assad's regime into the United States. In fact, the guidelines established by the Trump administration in its first one hundred days in power resulted in an increase in asylum cases; applicants were denied release under their own recognizance or with a bond, which meant longer periods of imprisonment as their applications were processed. Immigration lawyers have interpreted this action as a response to the president's failure to enact a "Muslim ban" through executive order.

One of the cases encompassed by these guidelines landed in Carlos Spector's office. On February 5, 2017, Mexican journalist Martín Méndez Pineda presented himself at the Juárez–El Paso border requesting asylum. He had been receiving death threats in the state of Guerrero after publishing an article describing various methods used by federal police officers to intimidate citizens. After presenting convincing evidence to establish "credible fear," ICE responded by denying his release from detention. According to Carlos, the U.S. government keeps asylum seekers locked up in detention for as long as possible in order to convince them to drop their asylum applications, which represents a grave danger for other journalists under threat in Mexico. In just the first four months of 2017, four journalists were murdered in Mexico, and two more were wounded but survived assassination attempts.

The first months of the Trump administration offered convincing evidence that its policies on asylum and detention of undocumented immigrants would not only seamlessly continue the policies established by the previous administration, which violated international humanitarian guidelines, but would also mean longer periods spent in detention. This would benefit the two large private companies that manage the country's immigrant detention facilities.

In the six months after Donald Trump won the presidential election on November 8, 2016, the stock prices of CoreCivic and GEO, the two largest operators of private immigrant detention centers, rose by over 100 percent. This was of course very good news for those companies, not only for the financial bonanza it represented, but because if things had gone in another direction, their futures would have been hanging by a thread.

On August 18, 2016, while Obama was still in office, Deputy Attorney General Sally Yates had ordered the Federal Bureau of Prisons to reduce the number of government contracts with private prisons. After that announcement, stock prices for both private prison corporations plummeted by 40 percent. Two months later, in the final days of the presidential campaign, Corrections Corporation of America (CCA) changed its name to CoreCivic and announced that it would have to make staff cuts in order to stay on budget. Trump and his adversary, Hillary Clinton, had made their opposing positions clear: Clinton vowed to cut private prison contracts, while Trump declared his conviction that the private prison system was good for the country.

Deputy Attorney General Yates's decision to cut back on private prison contracts was based on a Department of Justice report, which included an analysis of the drastic growth of the immigrant detention system in the United States. Between 1980 and 2013 it had grown by 800 percent and then decreased from 220,000 detainees in 2013 to 195,000 in 2016. Paying large sums of money to those private corporations was no longer necessary, the report concluded.

The two corporations' stunning rebound after the election—CoreCivic's stock rose 140 percent; GEO's rose 98 percent—took place against the backdrop of two situations. One was Trump's campaign rhetoric to lock up immigrants and the implicit need to keep the companies providing this service on the government payroll. The second was the donations that GEO and CoreCivic had made: $673,000 to the Republican Party and at least $130,000 to the Trump campaign.

On February 23, 2017, U.S. Attorney General Jeff Sessions rescinded Yates's memorandum, effectively breathing new life into CoreCivic and GEO. Sessions explained that maintaining private prison contracts would "meet the future needs" of the federal corrections system. Although Sessions's announcement did not directly allude to the detention of undocumented immigrants, then Secretary of Homeland Security John Kelly would refer to it explicitly three days later when he sent a memorandum to all agencies involved with immigration services and border security. The memo expanded the list of offenses to be considered crimes, which would also increase the number of undocumented people vulnerable to being arrested, detained, and put into deportation proceedings.

According to the memos signed by Kelly, the new administration would hire 15,000 new immigration agents to carry out these arrests; however, the memos authorized hiring only 50 new immigration judges. This meant that by mid-2017, 201 immigration judges would be handling over 500,000 pending cases, plus all the new cases for those detained during the new administration. There would be more detainees, a greater demand for private detention centers, longer waiting periods, and higher profits than ever for companies making a lucrative business of locking people up.

Trump had been in the Oval Office for less than a month when a series of photos taken by the Reuters news agency quickly traveled around the world. The pictures showed a family approaching the U.S. border, carrying their scant possessions in a few suitcases, holding their small children in their arms. They were trying to cross over, but not from Mexico into the United States. This family was fleeing the United States, trying to make it into Canada.

It would soon become clear that over the previous twelve months, coinciding with the beginning of the presidential campaign period in the United States and Republican candidate Trump's blatant anti-immigrant message, the number of people illegally crossing from this country into Canada in order to seek refuge or asylum had risen exponentially. The busiest area was the border with the Canadian province of Quebec; there, the number of people arrested for illegally crossing went from 254 in 2015 to 1,222 in 2016.

The average number of asylum applications per month at the land ports of entry in Quebec province rose from 111 in the first half of the year to 255 in September and 593 in December. These spikes followed Trump's July victory in the GOP primaries and his successful bid for the presidency in November. The total for 2016 was 1,695 applications, 72 percent up on the 985 registered in 2015. The trend continued into 2017 with a total of 3,365 asylum applications, twice the previous year's count.

According to Canada Border Services Agency (CBSA) records, most of those who illegally crossed from the United States to petition for asylum in the last months of 2017 and the beginning of 2017 were from Syria, Sudan, and Yemen, three of the seven nations included in Trump's "Muslim ban." In Manitoba, the majority were from Somalia, another of the seven nations. Other Canadian provinces, such as Manitoba and British Columbia, experienced the same phenomenon.

Although Canadian authorities have said they will not speculate on the possible motivations for this wave of migration, it is possible to infer that the measures adopted by the new U.S. presidential administration could be sending families to the northern border and into Canadian territory, where policies on refuge and asylum continue to be generous. Other asylum seekers do not even venture to present a petition for asylum in the United States, some activists explain, and go directly to Canada.

The democratic country that has long boasted of its tradition of opening its doors to "the huddled masses yearning to breathe free" has become a place that must be fled, a stepping-stone to somewhere else. Without laying a single brick, we've already built a wall.

When I began research for this book in 2013, Enrique Peña Nieto had just taken office as president of Mexico. Many victims of violence who had fled the country during Felipe Calderón's six-year term and his "war on narcotrafficking," with over 100,000 murders, including 48 journalists and 38 mayors killed, now hoped that with a new administration, the tide would turn and it would be safe for them to come home. That has not been the case. At the close of 2016, in Peña Nieto's fourth year in office, 67,000 people had been murdered during his term, including 30 journalists and 16 mayors. Indices of violence had risen in three out of four states. The brutal aggression in Mexico has not stopped. The corruption, massacres of civilians, and human rights violations continue to mount, while international organizations like Amnesty International, Human Rights Watch, and Reporters Without Borders grow weary of putting out recommendations that no one heeds.

In countries like Mexico, people are killed by impunity and the complicity of a state that does not meet its obligation to protect its own citizens. But there is complicity on the international level as well, where nations that boast of their welcoming, open arms make political use of humanitarian criteria, and respond to migrants with a cool pragmatism that turns to indifference and a lack of solidarity. People who live in those countries can choose to stop turning a blind eye, and begin to revise the laws and policies regarding mobility and migration—for economic or religious reasons, to save one's life, to seek a better life—from a global perspective. What has happened recently in the United States should serve as a call to action for all those living here who still believe in the dignity and strength of the human spirit. We must revise not only the process of arrival, but the criteria by which those who come here are considered worthy to stay. We must integrate into society those who have been victims, value their contributions to their new country, and support their efforts to rebuild their lives.

The political situation in the United States and the high visibility of migration on a global level—from Africa to Spain, from the Middle East to Germany, from Central America to the United States, from Haiti to South America—presents the ideal opportunity to redefine the concepts of citizenship and of borders, and the powers of those who govern nations without regard for the interests and will of the people. It is time to construct a new citizenship, to lay a foundation for the citizens to come, even the ones who knock down all of the walls.

# Notes

## 1. The Line Between Life and Death

1  Melissa del Bosque, "Cárteles y soldados en el lugar más peligroso de México," in *Cosecha roja*, August 5, 2012. Available at cosecharoja.org.
2  Although the U.S. Census gathers demographic data every five years, more recent figures for Fabens, Texas, were not available when this book went to press.

## 2. Carlos Spector, Attorney-at-Law for Impossible Cases

1  I spoke with Carlos Spector on this subject in 2013 and 2014, at the beginning of Mexican president Enrique Peña Nieto's six-year term in office. In the following years, as human rights violations have continued to take place, not only in Chihuahua but in other states such as Veracruz, where several journalists have been assassinated, and Guerrero, where forty-three students of the Ayotzinapa Rural College disappeared, denunciations from the international community have grown. But that has not resulted in a lessening of impunity throughout the country.
2  U.S. Department of Justice, Executive Office of Immigration Review, *Asylum Statistics FY 2012–2016*, March 2017. Available at justice.gov/eoir/file/asylum-statistics/download.
3  Galia García Palafox, "La mujer más valiente de México tiene miedo," *Gatopardo* 128 (February 2012). Available at gatopardo.com.

## 3. Constructing a Border

1 This discussion would reemerge front and center on the political scene and in public debate in 2016 with Donald Trump's presidential campaign. Although on numerous occasions experts and analysts concluded that construction of a border wall was untenable, based on a 2007 border wall initiative resulting in technical problems and budget shortfalls that prevented the project's completion, the wall became one of the Trump campaign's main talking points. After his inauguration in 2017, Trump had to concede that, in fact, there are technical limitations and budgetary constraints impeding construction.

2 These statistics came from the U.S. Customs and Border Protection website, but have since been deleted. The information was originally at https://www.cbp.gov/border-security/along-us-borders/border-construction/background-history-and-purpose/facts-figures.

## 4. Annunciation House: The Asylum Tradition

1 Séverine Durin, "Los que la guerra desplazó: familias del noreste de México en el exilio," *Desacatos* 38 (January–April 2012): 29–42. Centro de Investigaciones y Estudios Superiores en Antropología Social, Mexico. Available at redalyc.org.

## 5. Political Asylum: Sheltering Arms, But Not for Everyone

1 Jeffrey Passel and D'Vera Cohn, "Unauthorized Immigrant Population Stable for Half a Decade," Pew Research Center, September 2016. Available at pewresearch.org/fact-tank.

2 Jens Manuel Krogstad, Jeffrey Passel, and D'Vera Cohn, "5 Facts About Illegal Immigration in the U.S.," Pew Research Center, April 2017. Available at pewresearch.org/fact-tank.

3 Department of Homeland Security, *FY 2015 ICE Immigration Removals*, 2016. Available at ice.gov/removal-statistics.

4 David W. Haines, *Refugees in America in the 1990s: A Reference Handbook* (Westport, CT: Greenwood Press, 1996); Aviva Chomsky, *"They Take Our Jobs!" and 20 Other Myths About Immigration* (Boston: Beacon Press, 2007).

5   Chomsky, *"They Take Our Jobs!"*

6   This measure was revoked in early 2017, a few days before the end of Barack Obama's presidential term.

7   Bill Ong Hing, *Defining America Through Immigration Policy* (Philadelphia: Temple University Press, 2004).

8   Aviva Chomsky, *Undocumented: How Immigration Became Illegal* (Boston: Beacon Press, 2014).

9   Sarah Gammage, "El Salvador: Despite End to Civil War, Immigration Continues," Migration Information Source, July 2007, cited in Chomsky, *Undocumented*.

10  Michael McBride, "Migrants and Asylum Seekers: Policy Responses in the United States to Immigrants and Refugees from Central America and the Caribbean," *International Migration* 37, no. 1 (March 1999).

11  Hing, *Defining America Through Immigration Policy.*

12  Chomsky, *Undocumented.*

13  Ibid. In 1997 the Nicaraguan Adjustment and Central America Relief Act (NACARA) was passed in an attempt to clear the backlog of asylum cases, offering permanent residency to certain applicants from the region. Unfortunately the act sped up the process only for Nicaraguans and Cubans, while leaving Guatemalans and Salvadorans in limbo.

14  Another measure of this type, a palliative that provides only temporary relief, was announced in 2012 by President Barack Obama. Faced with insufficient support in the Republican-majority Congress for the DREAM Act, which would have granted permanent legal status to young undocumented immigrants who had been brought to the United States as children, the president passed a measure known as Deferred Action for Childhood Arrivals (DACA) through an executive action, without Congressional approval. Under certain criteria very similar to those of the DREAM Act, young immigrants were granted temporary status for two years, during which time they could receive temporary documents, including a work permit. But, just as with TPS, DACA beneficiaries do not have the option of applying for permanent residency or a pathway to citizenship.


## 6. Giving Up Freedom to Save Your Life

1   The visit to the detention center recounted here took place in February 2015, before CCA changed its name to CoreCivic in October 2016. The current name of the company is used throughout the text.

2   In April 2017, New York was the first state to establish a budget of $4 million to provide legal representation to undocumented immigrants.

These funds are administered by the New York Immigrant Family Unity Project (NYIFUP). See Vera Institute of Justice, "New York State Becomes First in the Nation to Provide Lawyers for All Immigrants Detained and Facing Deportation," April 7, 2017. Available at vera.org/newsroom/press-releases.

3  Maria M. Odom, *Annual Report 2015, Citizenship and Immigration Services*, USCIS, June 2015. Available at dhs.gov.
4  Ibid., 4.

## 9. Impunity

1  Charles Bowden, *Murder City: Ciudad Juárez and the Global Economy's New Killing Fields* (New York: Nation Books, 2010).
2  Sandra Rodríguez Nieto, *La Fábrica del crimen* (México, D. F.: Temas de hoy, 2012).
3  Ibid.
4  Ibid.

## 10. Seeking Justice from the Other Side

1  Transactional Records Access Clearinghouse, "Transfers of ICE Detainees from the Southwest Key Juvenile Center – Hacienda del Sol," Syracuse University, 2015. Available at trac.syr.edu.

## 11. Back to Life

1  In June 2015, a year and a half after this conversation, the mayor of Guadalupe at the time, Gabriel Urteaga Núñez, told the newspaper *Norte de Ciudad Juárez* that the population of Guadalupe was down to 1,500 people. In 2005, before Felipe Calderón took office, it had been 10,000.

## 12. The Never-Ending Wave

1  Diego Enrique Osorno, *La guerra de los Zetas* (New York: Vintage Español, 2013).
2  Mario Zúñiga Núñez, "Responsabilidad de Estados Unidos en el origen de las pandillas," in *El faro*, June 26, 2017. Available at elfaro.net.

3  Ibid.

4  Ibid.

5  U.S. Immigration and Customs Enforcement, "Statement of Thomas Homan, Executive Associate Director, Enforcement and Removal Operations, U.S. Immigration and Customs Enforcement, Department of Homeland Security, Regarding a Hearing on '*The Unaccompanied Children Crisis: Does the Administration Have a Plan to Stop the Border Surge and Adequately Monitor the Children?*' Before the U.S. Senate Committee on the Judiciary," February 23, 2016. Available at judiciary.senate.gov.

## 13. *"We Don't Want You Here!"*

1  The minor's name has been changed, and the name of her country of origin was omitted from legal documents to protect her identity.

2  Immigration Law Pocket Field Guide. "Nonimmigrant Clasifications", p. 53. LexisNexis, Charlottesville, VA. 2014.